THE CHURCH AND
YOUTH MINISTRY

The Church and Youth Ministry

Edited by Pete Ward

Published by Lynx Communications
Sandy Lane West, Oxford OX4 5HG
England
ISBN 0 7459 3224 X

Albatross Books Pty Ltd
PO Box 320, Sutherland
NSW 2232, Australia
ISBN 0 7324 1248 X

First edition 1995

ACKNOWLEDGMENTS

Scripture quotations taken from the Holy
Bible, New International Version. Copyright
© 1973, 1978, 1984 by International Bible
Society. Used by permission of Hodder &
Stoughton Ltd, a member of the Hodder
Headline Group.

Illustrations by Matthew Buckley

CONTENTS

LIST OF CONTRIBUTORS

John Allan is Chair of the Evangelical Alliance and Senior Youthworker at Belmont Chapel, Exeter.

Dave Astill is Parish Youthworker at St John's Church, Boscombe.

Colin Bennett is Lecturer in Youth Ministry at Moorlands Bible College.

Paul Borthwick is Minister of Missions, Grace Chapel, Lexington, United States.

Steve Gerali is Professor of Youth Ministry at Judson College, Chicago United States.

Simon Hall is Youthworker at Moretown Baptist Church.

Andy Hickford is Youth Minister at Stopsley Baptist Church, Luton, Executive Member of Brainstormers and Consultant Editor for *Youthwork* magazine.

David Howell is Director of Thamesdown Youth for Christ and Leadership Team Member of British Youth for Christ.

Fuzz Kitto is Youth Officer for the Synod Youth Unit, The Uniting Church of New South Wales, Australia.

Pete Ward is The Archbishop of Canterbury's Advisor for Youth Ministry, Tutor in Theology and Oxford Youthworks, and Honorary Research Fellow at the Centre for Theology and Education, Trinity College, Carmarthen.

FOREWORD

As we approach the end of this century, it is more important than ever that the church takes young people and youth culture seriously. I have often quoted the saying that 'the church is only ever one generation away from extinction', but the need for young people to be playing an active part in the life of the church is about much more than mere survival or numerical growth.

Historically, both in the church and outside it, young people have acted as agents of change. Their enthusiasm, freshness and vitality have often been the spur to spiritual renewal. At times, sadly, that enthusiasm has been dampened by others either through a refusal to change or from a fear of change. It is these issues, amongst others, that must be addressed if young people are to be enabled to play a proper role in the life of the church.

But change in the church should never be reckless or ill-considered. It needs to be backed by reflection, prayer and careful thought. For this reason, amongst others, I am delighted to commend the Lynx Youth Ministry Books as a useful tool to enable people to assess the process of change.

It is sad that we have sometimes thought of youth ministry as something which anyone can do without requiring any training or testing of their aptitude for the task. The demands now being made by the Children Act amongst other things are forcing us to look afresh at the particular skills needed by those caring for young people. In this context we should not ignore the many insights to be found in secular youthwork courses—nor should we be bound by them.

Christian youth ministry has its own characteristics. It is different from secular youth ministry. Whilst it is true that many of the core values of good Christian youthwork are by no means unique or particularly innovative, the timeless gospel of Christ needs to be proclaimed and incarnated afresh in every age and culture. In other words, it is itself subject to change.

Three particular areas stand out for me as ones that need to be urgently addressed:

The Bible: No one knows the full extent of the changes being brought about by the information technology revolution. More words are being produced than ever before—as are more video images—but the hunger I have seen for the Bible in many parts of the globe stands in stark contrast to the lack of enthusiasm for it in many parts of the Western world. The picture is made more complex still by the fact that many are no longer asking 'truth' questions. 'Does it work?' and 'How does it feel?' have often replaced the question 'Is it true?' Yet the latter is a question the Bible is constantly raising and is one we have to face for ourselves. Every youth minister needs to find ways of bringing this to young people within the context of their own culture. This is a daunting, but exhilarating, challenge and one which can be enormously rewarding when the Bible comes alive to a generation who often know little or nothing about it.

Worship: When I visited Taizé young people would often contrast the simplicity of the worship they experienced there with church services back at home. There was a simplicity about the worship of the brothers which spoke deeply to many of the 1,000 young people I travelled with. Yet part of the charm and power of the Taizé style of worship is the richness of the Christian tradition represented in their worship. The way that they use traditional words from the psalms and Christian liturgy, the use of icons and signs such as making a cross. For some of the young people from an evangelical tradition these ways of worship were new and strange, but many expressed their appreciation of them. Taizé in these ways points us to the truth that in looking for new forms of worship the Christian tradition is a rich, exciting resource.

Relationship: Community and fellowship are central to church life. Many young people are searching for a sense of identity and personhood. It is in relationship, firstly with God but also with each other, that we find ourselves to be who we are. If the church is to welcome young people then we need to find ways to build and foster relationships between adults and young people, because these relationships are the threads which bind the whole together. When I was in Durham, each summer members of the church would invite non-Christian people to go away on a sailing and canoeing holiday we called Watersports. In a relaxed atmosphere, through having fun together, we were able to share the Christian faith. Watersports was able to cross not only faith barriers but also generational ones as teenagers and older people within the church shared in Christian mission together. Now, I realize that an idea such as Watersports is not for everyone, yet in its emphasis upon relationships and friendship outreach surely it expresses a deep, enduring aspect of the gospel? Relationships are the context within which people find God and in doing so they also find themselves and each other. Relationships and the gospel, therefore, go hand in hand.

The church needs to find relevant and sustainable ways of building relationships with those young people who at present are socially and culturally excluded from the church. To do this we need committed people who have heard God's call to give themselves in relationship to young people.

These are some of the key areas youth ministers need to reflect on and it is my hope that this series will help to inspire a generation of such people to reach out in the name of Christ to young people.

ARCHBISHOP OF CANTERBURY

PREFACE

Christians have been involved in working with young people from the days that youthwork was invented. We have a long history of action, but we have been less impressive in developing a well-articulated and theologically informed body of knowledge. Most literature on Christian youthwork has been designed to provide quick solutions at an easy-to-use 'how to do it' level. Doing youthwork has always got to be primary, but the lack of any serious consideration of practice could be a fatal long-term weakness.

The Lynx Youth Ministry Books aim to provide a forum where the theory of youth ministry can be discussed. The first two volumes, *Relational Youthwork* and *The Church and Youth Ministry*, present a series of articles specially written for the series. The intention has been to gather a diversity of views in a single volume to foster further discussion and debate rather than to set down the definitive word on any subject. The authors discuss Christian work amongst young people from a variety of perspectives. Their views are, of course, their own, rather than those of the editor or of Lynx Communications.

The volumes are designed for use in the training of youthworkers and clergy as well as being accessible for those who wish to keep informed as to developments within youth ministry. The material is presented at a basic academic level. A number of the papers in these volumes were presented at the Conference for Youth Ministry held at Mansfield College, Oxford in January 1995.

PETE WARD, OXFORD 1995

1

The organization of youth ministries in the local church

JOHN ALLAN

Introduction

In a recent issue of *Youthwork* magazine, the veteran youthworker Wayne Rice remarked that two kinds of people were necessary for a local church's work amongst young people to be effective. One was the youthworker. The other—who might well have slightly different gifts and skills—was the person who organized the youthwork programme.

I believe this is absolutely true. Seven years ago I moved from the role of itinerant youth evangelist to begin work amongst the young people of a large Exeter evangelical church. I already knew a fair bit about youthwork, and I don't think many of my perceptions have changed since. Most of what I've learned in the past seven years has been about organization.

It is not enough for a church simply to have good, committed, trained and enthusiastic youthworkers. Often their work will never reach maximum effectiveness—or it will spurt, fizzle and die—unless it is contained within a structure that makes sense of it, maximizes its impact and prolongs its effect. All too often, the church which has a promising youthwork programme today will have lost it tomorrow, simply because the structure worked against its continuance, rather than supporting it. Structures can support life, or stifle it. As a hospital manager in our church is fond of saying, there isn't much difference between a lumbar support and a strait-jacket. But that difference is crucial.

One worrying trend of the past few years has ben that youthworkers tend to spend only twelve to eighteen months in the job before resigning, which can create haphazard variations in quality. We need to develop structures in our local church youth programmes which encourage continuity and consistency. (And perhaps entice people to stay around a little longer too.) The old days of flying by the seat of our pants must now be over. We need a set of structures for our youthwork which will be solidly based, designed for cultural appropriateness and deeply rooted in biblical values.

How things have changed

It isn't so long ago that it was possible for effective youthwork to be carried on in an instinctive, unreflective way. Building and shaping a large, lively youth group wasn't so difficult, if you had a heart for kids and a gut feeling for how to go about it. For a whole variety of factors, this is no longer the case.

First, the instability of relationships in our society means that young people make more demands on the significant relationships in their lives. They are less prone to trust adults easily; they find it safer to relate to us as 'consumers' of whatever product we are offering, than as real friends and confidants. It's not as easy to build relationships with young people as it used to be; they are skilled at holding us off at arm's length. It takes more time and involvement to travel the same distance. Haphazard structuring may mean that we spend all of our time in secondary activities, rather than maximizing the time we have available to develop relationships.

Second, because of this, small-scale work has become much more the order of the day. Gone are the massive, thriving youth clubs of the past, where the sheer numbers ensured incredible momentum. More and more, our best work is done amongst the little groups, the 'clusters', and this entails the greater organization of a larger team.

In addition, people now have increased expectations of church programmes. It used to be possible to govern our church via a monthly elders' meeting which took care of all significant business. Now we have a leadership team meeting every fortnight, with five other 'functional teams' taking on much of the workload which used to be the brief of the old elders. Why? Because, in common with most other churches, our range of activities has greatly increased.

Says Steve Gaukroger: 'Somehow, people have come to expect that all their needs—social, physical, emotional, spiritual—will be met by the church... Perhaps our churches are so often characterized by a lack of gratitude because we assume that pastoral care is a right that we should expect, rather than a privilege for us to enjoy.'

Young people who watch MTV, rent multimillion-budget videos, and attend concerts with stunning light shows and visual effects are unlikely to be attracted by the offer of bright singing and a glass of orange squash. We may not be able to do everything—but what we do do must be done well.

So we must ask the question: what are the essentials of a properly planned approach? What kinds of work should a church be doing?

It goes without saying (I hope) that there is no one blueprint for local church youthwork. There's a wide spectrum of possibilities, some of which will work in one situation, some in another.

But however different our philosophies of ministry may be, it is important to see that ultimately they are all serving the same ends. The main purposes of local church youthwork do not vary. They can be summed up in terms of the gifts listed by Paul in Ephesians 4:11–13, where he divides the 'grace' Christ has given to the church into five areas which taken together produce in us 'the whole measure of the fulness of Christ'.

'Apostles' and 'prophets' are less important for our present purposes. It is certainly true that our youthwork needs to be 'apostolic', always looking for new opportunities, always seeking to plant where no one has gone before. The local church youthwork which becomes predictable, boring and introverted loses its drive and dynamic very quickly. And we need to be 'prophets'. Our youthwork needs to be constantly speaking the present mind of God, alerting his people to where the Spirit is at work, never trapped in a rut but constantly responsive to the movement of God's breath amongst us. But the key ministries for local church work will probably be those of 'evangelist', 'pastor' and 'teacher'. Whatever our programme of youthwork, all three elements must be there.

(There will be times, of course, when one of the three assumes more importance than the other two. It depends on our precise situation. Nevertheless, in healthy youthwork, all three will be present in some shape or form.)

Evangelism

As we work out our strategy for evangelism, there are three points to bear in mind. First, different young people will be reached by different means. Many young people who do not come from Christian backgrounds, but are like the Christians in outlook, social class, aspirations and moral behaviour, will readily become Christians through the witness of their friends.

But nine out of ten kids aren't like that! And because of their distance from the Christian consensus, enabling young adults are likely to make more impact upon them than teenage Christians can. If our evangelism is based on events to which our existing group will bring their friends, we will be reproducing our group in its own image—no bad thing, if there are lots of kids like our own to be won. But in a society where the number of 'C kids' is ever more rapidly increasing, the wise youthwork organizer will ask whether or not God has a more radical evangelistic strategy in mind.

Second, evangelism is not one activity. For many years we have assumed that it is; for instance, we have laid on a 'gospel concert', and relied upon this single event to introduce people to our midst, teach them the salient points of our message and induce in them a psychological crisis leading to conversion! Rather a lot of expectations to place upon one evening, especially when teenagers are becoming arch-consumers, able to extract what they want to receive from what we offer, and politely discard the rest.

I believe that in what we call 'evangelism' there are actually three activities going on together. One is attracting the attention of young people; big-scale, ambitious events are a good way of making teenagers turn their heads and begin to consider what we are saying. But although this may impress them, it shouldn't be confused with 'evangelism'. It needs to be followed by a second activity: teaching. If it is true that most people in the United Kingdom today need to hear the gospel at least five times before they can begin to make sense of it, then we must no longer expect teenagers to respond genuinely and effectively to Jesus the first time they hear an appeal. We need to give them a clear picture of what precisely is being offered, and what demanded; what are the attractions, and what are the costs of the lifetime of discipleship to which they are being summoned. An emotional exhortation may produce a response, but it won't be a lasting one.

Then, third, there needs to be an appeal to decide. Young people are capable of putting off decisions forever unless they are confronted forcibly with the need to make up their minds. And so we need to weave into our programme natural opportunities for decision points and growth opportunities—house parties, weekends, visits to evangelistic events, personal chats with the leader.

A well-organized local church youth ministry will not put all of its evangelistic eggs into one basket. Its annual programme will blend together all three activities in a way which enables young people to progress naturally from one stage of involvement to the next.

Another vital point is that evangelism needs to merge into effective discipling. Sometimes it is hard to tell where one ends and the other begins; teenagers are so volatile, so unpredictable, that we often cannot tell (and often they cannot) whether or not the grace of God has actually taken hold of their lives or not. But effective evangelism is not over until a discipling process has begun which addresses all three areas of the teenager's personality: mind, will and emotions.

Traditionally we have been good at informing the mind—confronting the new believer with Christian doctrine, and teaching all the things a Christian needs to know. But learning is just one of the key activities in discipleship. The others are living, which is where the will comes in—beginning to put into practice all the things which are being mentally absorbed, in a way which has an impact upon the lifestyle; and loving, which involves our relationships both with others and with God. Learning to love our Father, and express that love in worship, goes alongside learning to love our brothers and sisters.

Local church discipleship programmes for teenagers tend to be more heavily biased towards one area than another. Many charismatic ministries stress the relational, emotional side of growing in Christ, with the result that teenagers find it hard to sustain the long haul when problems come. More Reformed approaches stress the submission of the will, and produce correct, disciplined, but joyless Christianity. Others of us teach lots of doctrine, and inform the mind without affecting the behaviour. A well-organized youth ministry will concentrate on balancing its emphases.

Teaching

What do we need to remember in structuring our teaching ministry with young people? First, that learning is more than absorbing facts. We are trying to instill three things: knowledge, skills and attitudes. It isn't just a matter of knowing the truth, but of having the skills to apply it in our lives—in church life, in interpersonal relationships, in service for God. And neither knowledge nor skills will be much use without the attitudes which prompt us to make use of them. Our training needs to be biblical (knowledge), but also practical (skills) and motivational (attitudes). Organizing youth ministry means developing ways of encouraging all three types of learning.

Second, we must remember that learning is progressive. New discoveries are made on the basis of what is already appreciated. For this reason, it is vital that our teaching curriculum is purposeful and well integrated with what our young people will have picked up before they come to us. We need to have a system of goals and expectations which allows us to monitor just how effective our teaching really is.

Third, the best teaching opportunities are often the unstructured ones. We frequently communicate more through the informal, life-on-life exchanges which take place naturally through spending time together rather than through the carefully designed programmes over which we spend hours of preparation time! And this was the style of the rabbis, which was the style of Jesus himself. Wise youthwork planners will recognize the importance of this teaching element in the way they plan their workers' use of time.

Fourth, some young people will learn faster than others. This is why our strategy needs to incorporate the concept of a 'core' group, in which those who are on the 'fast track' can encourage one another, grow up in Christ and provide a stimulus to the others. Insisting that everyone learn at the same speed is simply inviting frustration and defection, since you aren't supplying the needs of anyone, but only of the mythical 'average' person.

Fifth, it is important for young people to have at their disposal the resources of the whole church. No one youthworker can meet all the teaching needs of the young people; and in fact God has placed many kinds of gifts in the church, precisely to meet those situations which the youthworker is not gifted to cover. And so part of our strategy must be to bring our young people together with older church members in a context where each can appreciate the other; where young can encourage old (1 Timothy 4:12) and old can instruct young. The youthworker should not act as a fount of all wisdom to the teenagers in his or her charge; but rather as a matchmaker, bringing together two unwilling parties who are going to fall in love with each other!

Finally, teaching is not complete until pupils have learned to instruct themselves. The aim of all our teaching should be to reach the point where our young people are able to feed themselves. And so the arrangement of our curriculum needs to lead towards independence in personal study habits. If our young people pass from our hands still dependent on someone else to explain the word of God to them, how will they survive as adult Christians?

Pastoring

The third main area of local church youth ministry is pastoring. What principles should guide our organization here?

First, the importance of one-to-one counselling. It is vital to organize our work in such a way that young people have natural, unembarrassing opportunities to come and talk to us. The more barriers we impose between them and our office/study, the less effective our work is going to be. Duffy

Robbins has written (for example) about the 'open door myth', the idea that if we keep our door permanently open to young people, they will come seeking help. In fact, they may be daunted; if our room is always full of other kids hanging about, they may feel unwilling to come and broach anything too personal or intimate.

Second, the centrality of the group's life. Lawrence Richards has warned that a teen ministry based on counselling is 'doomed to failure'. This is because teenagers are herd animals, and peer pressure is one of the most important facts of life. The only Christian teenagers who are likely to stand are those whose testimony is affirmed and encouraged by a peer group of believers like themselves. Pastoral organization of the youth group entails teaching them to support one another, rather than being constantly driven by adults.

But, third, adult resources—other than the 'official' leadership—are extremely important. Good organization means creating the set of conditions in which adults in the church feel a pastoral responsibility for teenagers who do not belong to their family; and where teenagers feel close enough to non-related adults that they can go to see them with their problems and questions. 'The whole church does youthwork', as Winkie Pratney puts it; only in an unhealthy church is youthwork left to the youthworkers.

Finally, individual accountability is the heart of all pastoral encouragement. If the young person feels that no one would notice if she stopped coming, she will stop coming. There can be different structures to bring about accountability: in some groups it is understood that everyone will have a six-monthly 'check-up' with the youth pastor; in others, a structure of small, intimate 'cell groups' breaks down the impersonality of the large youth group. But whatever the structure, the principle remains the same: when we feel someone is watching, and caring, we make progress much more quickly.

Conclusions

To be a good youthworker demands a rare mix of skills and abilities. To be a good organizer of youthwork demands far more: everything that is involved in being a good youthworker, plus a grasp of strategic planning, an ability to see the total profile of a work and its forward thrust, enough diplomatic skill to relate well to adults in the church and especially the church's leadership, a restlessly creative and absorbent mind, the spiritual insight to discern the will of God and the stamina to keep going over a long period.

In too many churches, the shape of youth ministry is largely unplanned. It reflects the particular emphases and enthusiasms of whoever happens to be in charge of youthwork at the time; it is unbalanced, it neglects vital emphases; and it never outlives the people who brought it into being.

In other churches, the strategy of youth ministry is determined by the leadership team, the vicar, the church council or the deacons. None of these may have any recent hands-on experience of youthwork, or any up-to-date understanding of the needs and dilemmas of young people.

Over the past few years in this country, we have begun at last to see the need for proper training and development of youthworkers. But surely there is an equal need—if not a more pressing one—to train and inform the minds of those whose job it is to supervise the whole process? Otherwise, the new wine is simply being poured into old bottles. And old bottles split.

2

Shifting paradigms in youth ministry

FUZZ KITTO

In Australia, the United Kingdom, Canada, the United States, and in much of the Western world, the time when Christendom had major influence is past. The time of mission and the emerging mission field has arrived.

William Willimon and Stanley Hauerwas tell of the day in 1963 when Christendom died in Greenville, South Carolina.[1] On that day the Fox Theatre opened on a Sunday, and the senior Sunday School class was seen to quietly slip out of the back door of the church to join John Wayne on the big screen. For me, the day of Christendom died when I was sixteen years old. Some of my church leaders told me to keep away from the kids that were not acceptable—after a worship service where the Bible reading was about Jesus mixing with tax collectors and prostitutes. I was told that if they were not willing to come to church, I should not spend my time trying to help them.

Loren Mead, in *The Once and Future Church*, observes two past paradigms of the church. The first, the 'apostolic paradigm', held from the first generations after Jesus to the conversion of Constantine. Here, Mead observes, the church had a diversity of style and structure, appropriate to varying contexts. It lived in a context that was basically hostile. It had a strong sense of being called, and of being sent to serve and convert the world with compassion and love. Its central reality was a local community that was 'called out' of the world, distinctive from the world but still a part of it; its call was to engage with the world, not to retire from it (in the world but not of the world). It had a strong sense of mission and the mission frontiers were right outside the doors of the church. It 'perceived that the meaning of its life was to build up its members with the courage, strength, and skill to communicate God's good news within that hostile world'.[2] It was an intimate community, whose spirit demanded that it serve and care for a world antagonistic to itself.

The second, Mead calls the 'Christendom paradigm'. It began with the conversion of the Roman Emperor in AD 313 and instead of taking generations to emerge (as did the apostolic paradigm) the change took centuries. By law the church was associated with the empire. The world immediately surrounding the church was legally associated with the church. Congregations and communities were replaced by geographically defined parishes, and individual Christians were no longer called to witness in a hostile world. The frontiers of the mission were the frontiers of the empire and therefore left to 'professionals' to undertake. Mission became a 'far-off enterprise', which was a part of the foreign policy of the nation/empire and linked to colonialism.

Unity became a key objective of the church because the size of the church (and the empire) was such that it had to be managed. This could only be done if there was a strong sense of commitment to commonality, standard structures and diminished discord. What eventually emerged to provide this structure was the denomination. Denominations arose, mirroring the structure of the nation or empire that they were subsumed in. David Bosch, in his book on paradigms of the church and its mission, observes that the structure of the church always mirrors the structure of the society in which it finds itself and that theology always grows out of mission.[3]

In the Australian context, Arthur Philip, the first governor, along with his officers, was known to feel disdain for the consolations of religion, but to see it as an important social utility. The evangelical first chaplain was also seen to be useful for his religious emphasis in that he preached in favour of subordination, and against drunkenness, whoring and gambling, making him the natural moral policeman in the new settlement.[4] Again, this operated within the Christendom view that the church and the state worked together in helping make the kingdom come—even if this was not the reality!

In the Christendom paradigm the church determined the framework for the community, for living, and the structure for social conformity. We know that this is no longer so. Kennon Callahan, a church-planning consultant, tells of a discussion with Peter Drucker at a conference in 1991 on: 'Where is the church headed in the twenty-first century?' Drucker postulated that the decline in religion was due to two things: the decline in social conformity and the increase in the freedom of choice.[5] Declines in social conformity and freedom of choice are two major contributing factors to the emergence of youth, and particularly youth cultures, since World War 2. In fact, some would argue that youth culture came about because of young people being separated from other generations, thereby allowing them to discover the freedom to choose and follow differing paths, values and lifestyles from those of their parents, and the norms of the dominant culture. The emerging social norms and realities no longer included church, youth group or Sunday School. Meanwhile, all these programmes continue to attempt to live out traditions and create conformities that are increasingly removed from the everyday life of the majority of the population.

The Australian National Church Life Survey (which surveyed more than 310,000 church attendees from 6,700 churches in nineteen Protestant denominations) shows clear differences in religious consciousness between those born before World War 2 and those born afterwards. The differences range from the way they read the Bible to their view on and practice of speaking in tongues; from the way they worship to the way they share their faith. Perhaps the most telling was the response to the question: 'How important is lifelong affiliation to a denomination?' Amongst those born before World War 2 it was important to 45 per cent of respondents, while to those born after World War 2 it was only important to 15 per cent.[6] The day of the denomination offering programmes and a youth ministry structure in which people automatically want to play a part is clearly over. Lyle Schaller, in *Twenty-one Bridges to the Twenty-first Century*, sees the role of the denominations shifting to a more grass-roots level with a local congregation emphasis becoming essential as each congregation seeks to relate to, and be on mission in, its unique mission field.[7]

Certainly since World War 2, with increased numbers of young people attending high school, and with increasingly age-graded classes, young people have had the encouragement and the confidence to explore being different. Along with this, the change in education from 'jug in mug' to exploring answers for themselves, and the stress on the individual, have all given credence to young people exploring freedom in a climate of a general decline in social conformity.

Ronald Koteskey, in his chapter 'Adolescence as a Cultural Invention' in *Handbook of Youth Ministry*, argues that societies which have created adolescence and increased its span (with lower ages of puberty and higher ages of adulthood) have created distinctive problems. These range from not giving young people an identity in our culture and forbidding marriage when they reach puberty (but giving little help on what to do with their sexuality) to making it illegal or difficult to work while forcing them to spend time in school.[8] There are also problems for youth, created by the conscription of the majority into the lower strata of a meritocratic educational system which then trains them for occupations which are meaningless, poorly paid and uncreative. Youth, or at least young people, is not a problem, although some of the youth subcultures may be seen as a threat.[9]

All this has vast implications for the way in which young people view themselves, God and the church. Youth ministry has its roots in the image of young people or youth as a problem. Many would argue that youth came into existence because of given socio-political forces in different societies. In the United Kingdom, for instance, children were removed from mines and workhouses; and in the United States, many forces were at work to get young people out of factories and off farms, helping to create a labour shortage in what had become a labour surplus because of industrialization, increased immigration, urbanization, increased mobility and other factors.

In Australia, the roots of adolescence could be argued to be in the formation of what became known as the 'currency kids'. These were the children of the convicts; they were the first true white Australians. These kids were often also illegitimate. Catholics, for instance, could not marry in the early years of the colony because there was no official Catholic priest. This was despite the fact that more than one-third of the colony were Irish Catholics.[10] These 'currency kids' were left, on the whole, to roam by themselves. They formed their own values, social system and accent, distinctive from the officers, civil servants and even their own parents. To the church they were a source of deep concern—indeed, they were a problem.

In each nation, the church took initiatives to try to overcome this problem by educating the young people as a means of saving them from the temptations of idleness. There was also a pervading belief that by developing literacy, it would lead to them reading the scriptures and Christian tracts for themselves, they would become good Christians and, therefore, good citizens. Here developed the emphasis and underlying assumption that the basis for good Christian work with young people is education.

This paralleled the attitude and assumptions on which most mission work with Australian Aboriginal people was based. It was extended a little but the attitude was to treat Aborigines like young people. The main mission strategy was to try to educate them to be civilized by putting them in schools. Some who were younger were taken away from their old people so that they would not be able to induct them into the old ways and to socialize them into the Aboriginal culture. As John Harris notes in *One Blood*: 'With a few notable exceptions... most missionaries until very recently found very little which was worthwhile in Aboriginal culture.'[11] It was a form of enculturation—often done with the greatest love and concern, but still a form of missioning that assumed that within the civilized English culture the kingdom of God had surely come. In this churched culture—it was indeed ethnocentric—they found it difficult to separate culture from faith. Because faith came in cultural baggage it was difficult ever to develop indigenous missioning, worship and structures. Coming out of the same paradigm youth ministry, therefore, became tied to teaching the norms of social conformity and cultural beliefs.

The church culture which grew out of the Christendom paradigm developed a style of youth ministry that was church-based. Primarily it concentrated on teaching the Bible and community customs, and aimed at holding young people in the church through fun, games, activities and group membership. Some have argued that it was a holding pattern. It seemed that the aim was to maintain interest in coming to church, or at least church buildings, until they became adults and could become real Christians. Others, however, used what has been called the 'Mary and her little lambs' approach, where if you leave them alone, they will eventually come home; home, here, being the church.

The other anomaly which grew out of the more recent church culture was the professional youthworker, who would work out there with those other young people outside the church. They did the frontier youthwork for the church as it started to notice that the frontiers were getting closer to their doors. Many times a rift was caused between the community and the church. These youthworkers became known in many areas as detached youthworkers. So youthworkers would either become churched-based or community-based, working with those who were in or with those who were out. A tension for youthworkers has been that they have often wanted to work with both. The Christendom paradigm does not easily allow for this. What worked in Christendom worked for Christendom, but does not work anymore.

The time we are now in is a time between paradigms. It is like post-modernism in that we know what we are not, but are not yet convinced of what we are. As Loren Mead reminds us, 'With each change of paradigm, roles and relationship change and power shifts. New structures develop. New directions emerge. Things that were of great value in one age become useless in the next. Times of transition between ages and paradigms are times of confusion and tumult. A new paradigm always emerges from the church's new sense of its mission.'[12]

The way in which we discover our new sense of mission in youth ministry is by explaining youth culture, in other words by contextualizing. Youth has been an important area of study for many social researchers, particularly for the purposes of advertising, so there are often reports done on youth cultures.

Hugh Mackay is one of Australia's most noted social researchers and in his reports on young Australians—ten- to eighteen-year-olds, and teenagers and their parents— asked young people: 'What does it feel like to be a teenager in Australia?'[13] The responses included recognition that more options existed for them than for their parents, but that this brought more pressure and risk to their lives. Security was described in terms of belonging to the group; conformity and moral responsibility to the group were found to be much stronger than conformity to the community. Many found difficulty in establishing an ethical framework that had any relevance beyond their immediate peer relationship circle. Boredom was seen to be the great enemy.

Richard Eckersley, another researcher, policy consultant and futurologist with the Australian federal government, has done extensive research into the dilemma of young people, particularly for the Australian Commission for the Future. Eckersley claims that young people in Australia are being afflicted by 'cultural abuse'. He cites the key issues affecting young people as: suicide; unemployment; drugs; the rise of eating disorders, particularly amongst young females; mental disorders; and crime.[14] He goes on to say: 'Our culture arguably fails to meet the most fundamental requirements of any culture: to provide a sense of belonging and purpose and so a sense of meaning and self-worth, and a moral framework to guide our conduct.'[15]

In our research through Our God Cares work in our youth unit, we discovered that the key concerns, in order of frequency, are: boredom/nothing to do; drugs; alcohol; violence; crime; unemployment; transport; and environ- mental issues. We asked young people: 'What do you think young people in this area most want out of life?' To this, they responded, in order of priority: a good time; a good job; good education; happy relationships; financial security; to travel; and to own their own home. We have observed four trends which have emerged over the past ten years:

⊙ a 'me' orientation—not so much out of selfishness but survival;

⊙ a loss of purpose and meaning;

⊙ feelings of a loss of power; and

⊙ a sense of the absence of future or hope.[16]

From this exegesis of youth culture it emerges that, rather than youth being seen as a problem, the things that matter to young people—and that perhaps they look to religion to provide—include:

⊙ the search for identity;

⊙ the search for meaning and purpose;

⊙ the search for belonging or family; and

⊙ the search for a future.

These almost parallel what Kennon Callahan calls 'life searches'.[17] In the search for identity, it is helping young people to discover that they have the power to affect their own lives and future. In the search for meaning, it is to offer meaningful experiences and projects for young people to do which make a difference to the world, and to provide a sense that they can change the world. The search for belonging might mean helping the peer group to be a positive force and to extend the skills of being a community beyond the 'mono-cultural' group. In the search for a future, it is to demonstrate a sense of destiny and a power beyond themselves. Young people search for these things in all kinds of ways through all kinds of behaviours and, sadly, they sometimes give up.

Richard Eckersley, as an agnostic observer, reflected that there should be a role for religion, especially Christianity, in the task of remaking our culture.[18] Our role in the emerging paradigm is to help young people with these life searches. The time between paradigms, in which there is a state of flux as well as some confusion, as we seek to build the future rather than just to modify the past, is a time to experiment and discover what is effective. As William Easum wisely suggests, 'If churches only improve what they have been doing they will die... the best way to fail today is to improve yesterday's successes.'[19]

In some of the experimenting we have been doing over the past fifteen years particularly, we have made some discoveries. In working with second-generation, migrant, ethnic young people, we have discovered that it is possible to help them to create a new culture. We have also discovered that it is possible to redeem or convert a whole culture or subculture, rather than just individuals. This should not be surprising because the Old Testament in particular talks more of redeeming whole nations than it does of redeeming individuals.

In working with largely community welfare referred young people from working-class areas, we discovered that new congregations work best for new Christians and vice versa. Again, this should not be surprising because the first-century church was precisely this. Youth cultures are cultures of freedom and diversity, and give rise to many subcultures, each with its own ideas and values, conventions and characteristics, decision-making and leadership, meeting places, argot and communication, and hopes for the future. Each of these contexts can authentically develop its own distinctive, indigenous Christianity. Working in a prison, we discovered that the mission team members did not need to have it all together, to know everything about the faith or even to be totally sure of it.

Unlike missionaries who went to Africa in past centuries with their coffins, because they were so convinced of their faith that they went knowing that they would not return, mission team members today discover their faith as they are forced to express it. Perhaps this is also the basis of the success of work camps in the United States.

So we have some clues about possible future directions. Let us clarify and contrast the difference between Christian youthwork in a mission culture and a churched culture:

⊙ In a mission culture, the emphasis is on developing relationships. The basis of any effective mission or ministry with young people is relationships. About 86 per cent of people who have come to faith in Australia did so because of Christian friends or family. Jesus himself modelled a relational approach in almost all contexts. The young people we surveyed in our research with high-school students across Australia (a sample of about 6,000) put 'being a good friend' as one of their top life-time desires. Tom Zanzig refers to relational ministry as the first stage of ministry. It is the building of relationships of trust upon which all further ministry must be based.[20]

⊙ In a mission culture, the focus is on faith sharing. Faith in most situations is caught, not taught! We have found in much of our evangelism that young people see the gospel before they hear it. Through story, lifestyle, justice, compassion and proclamation, faith can be communicated in terms and images which touch the spirit and enliven the mind. An old South American saying goes: 'Don't tell me what you believe. Let me observe you and then I will tell you what you believe.'

⊙ In a mission culture, the focus is in the world. Rather than creating Christian ghettos inside the church, the world becomes the focus. People live their lives as Christians in the world. God is already in the world. In a mission culture, it is recognized that young people live in many cultures and subcultures. Choice, change and diversity are traits of the age, and immigration has created a plethora of ethnic-based cultures. As Marina Herrera reminds us, youth ministry must also have a direct multicultural dimension when intended for youth in the dominant culture.[21] Within the dominant culture there are many subcultures. Subcultures call into question the adequacy of the dominant cultural ideology. What does the Australian way of life offer to a Vietnamese young person living in the western suburbs of Sydney? There is now no such thing as 'a' youth culture. Coca-Cola no longer makes one advertisement aimed at young people, but makes many.

⊙ In a mission culture, young people are offered a future, meaning, identity and belonging—because these are the basic yearnings and life searches.

⊙ In a mission culture, it is assumed that young people are searching for spirituality. This concept was not new to the apostle Paul on Mars Hill in Acts 17. Paul explained to the Greeks the basis of their pagan culture, and showed them clearly their search for God and the spirituality that led them to build an altar to an unknown God. In a mission culture, we learn young people's language, images of God, faith and self, and we look for entry points to the gospel. These are missionary tasks.

⊙ In a mission culture, leadership is by giftedness and competency. It just does not work any other way in a mission culture; you cannot get away with leadership unless it is competent.

⊙ In a churched culture, the focus is on good programmes. The understanding in a church culture is that young people really want to come to church. All you have to do is to put on good programmes to attract them.

⊙ In a churched culture, the focus is on Christian education. Christian education becomes the process of learning the community's values, teachings, customs and social norms.

⊙ In a churched culture, the focus is in the church. The belief is that people need to come into the church because God is found in the church. The world is sinful; coming to church continues to redeem us, and to renew us as the focus for grace and the means of grace.

⊙ In a churched culture, it is mostly assumed that young people live in a similar culture. Their world becomes the world. It assumes that young people make the transition easily or at least can if they try. Therefore, 'a' youth programme will be relevant for all.

⊙ In a churched culture, the offering is doctrine, education and tradition. The underlying assumption is that if young people could but learn the doctrines and traditions, then they could find God.

⊙ In a churched culture, it is assumed that young people want to be Christians and a part of the church, or are rebelling against it.

⊙ In a churched culture, it is assumed that young people have some understanding of the biblical concepts of God and religious language.

⊙ In a churched culture, leadership is by age, position and the number of degrees one has.

We are now moving into a new paradigm. In our team, we have come to describe this time as a time of choice, change and diversity. Choice—where people expect to make their own decisions. Change—where there is a certainty that the future is changing and the past is no longer a helpful guide. Diversity—where there are a range of options in every facet of life.[22]

A joke is told of an Australian eight-seater aeroplane which crashed into an Australian cemetery—at the last count they had recovered 155 bodies. Many times, it is not just what happens that matters, but where it happens. The context, time and motivation cause us to have insights into how to be proactive rather than reactive, and how to read the context in order to determine the mission and then to translate and plant the gospel in this new ground. But it is still God who is there causing it. One of the great missioners said: 'I planted the seed, Apollo watered the plant, but it was God who made the plant grow. The one who plants and the one who waters really do not matter. It is God who matters, because it is God who makes the plant grow' (1 Corinthians 3:6,7).

NOTES

1. W. Willimon and S. Hauerwas.

2. Loren Mead, *The Once and Future Church*, The Alban Institute, 1991.

3. David Bosch, *Transforming Mission: Paradigm Shifts in Theology of Mission*, Orbis, 1991.

4. Manning Clark, *A Short History of Australia*, The New American Library, 1963.

5. Kennon Callahan, *Dynamic Worship*, Harper San Francisco, 1994

6. Pater Kaldor, *et al*, *Winds of Change: The Experience of Church in a Changing Australia*, Anzea, 1994.

7. Lyle Schaller, *Twenty-one Bridges to the Twenty-first Century*, Abingdon, 1994.

8. Donald Ratcliff and James A. Davies (eds), *Handbook of Youth Ministry*, REP Books, 1991.

9. Michael Brake, *Comparative Youth Culture*, Routledge, 1985.

10. Ian Breward, *A History of the Australian Churches*, Allen and Unwin, 1993.

11. John Harris, *One Blood: 200 years of Aboriginal Encounter with Christianity: A Story of Hope*, Albatross, 1990.

12. Mead, *The Once and Future Church*.

13. Hugh Mackay, *The Mackay Report: Teenagers and their Families*, Mackay Research, 1988; Hugh Mackay, *The Mackay Report: Young People in Australia*, Mackay Research, 1989.

14. Richard Eckersley, *The Challenges to Change*, Commission for the Future, Australian Government Publishers, 1992.

15. Richard Eckersley, 'Failing a Generation: The Impact of Culture on the Health and Well-Being of Youth', a paper presented to the Australian Rotary Health Research Fund Fifth International Conference, November 1992.

16. Fuzz and Carolyn Kitto (eds), *Trends for Youthworkers*, from an interview with Richard Eckersley, Joint Board of Christian Education, May 1993 edition.

17. Kennon Callahan, *Effective Church Leadership*, San Francisco, Harper and Row, 1990.

18. Fuzz Kitto, from an unpublished paper 'Trends in Youth Cultures in Australia', 1993.

19. William Easum, *Dancing with Dinosaurs: Ministry in a Hostile and Hurting World*, Abingdon Press, 1993.

20. Michael Warren (ed.), *Readings and Resources in Youth Ministry*, Saint Mary's Press, 1987, p. 43.

21. Compiled by John Roberto, *Readings in Youth Ministry Volume 1: Foundations*, National Federation for Catholic Youth Ministry, 1986.

22. Dean Drayton, Carolyn Kitto and David Manton, *Planning for Mission*, Uniting Church NSW Board of Mission, 1993.

23. Adapted from the Good News Bible, Australian Edition, 1988.

OTHER SOURCES

Rolland Allan, *Missionary Methods: St Paul's or Ours*, Eerdmans, 1962.

David Maunders, *Keeping Them Off the Streets*, Philip Institute of Technology, 1984.

Faith Popcorn, *The Popcorn Report*, Random House Australia, 1991.

Jim Punton, *The Messiah People: Punton Papers Volume 1*, Hot Iron Press, 1978.

Quentin Schultze, et al, *Dancing in the Dark: Youth, Popular Culture, and the Electronic Media*, Eerdmans, 1991.

3

Distance and closeness: finding the right ecclesial context for youthwork

PETE WARD

How Christian youthwork relates to the church is one of the key areas for discussion at this time. Central to this debate is the question of how closely linked or how distant youth ministry needs to be to work most effectively. Recent trends within UK church life have tended to move youthwork much closer to the congregational life. Whilst 'open youthwork' with those outside the church has declined, the numbers of full-time youth ministers working mainly with Christian groups in churches has mushroomed. The present emphasis upon the family in evangelical church life has tended to focus attention on attendance at one 'family worship time'. Moreover, recent developments in thinking about outreach, such as Robert Warren's concern to develop missionary congregations and the ideas from Willow Creek, have tended to focus attention on how the whole congregation together needs to engage in outreach.[1]

Whilst mainstream youth ministry is, generally speaking, in the grip of current centripetal tendencies exhibited by the church, there are indications that something of a break-out is on its way. All over the United Kingdom, groups of young people and young adults are starting to experiment with new approaches to worship. Organizationally, such initiatives may have a variety of different relationships to the church; however, some sort of distance from the church is implied in each of these developments. Distance, firstly, is focused on the issue of culture and worship, because these services generally arise from a realization that mainstream church life is culturally divorced from young people. Most groups therefore have found that a separate service is needed in order to gain a distinct 'cultural space' where worship can be developed which arises from popular culture.

Alongside the growth of new forms of worship there is a parallel, and sometimes linked, tendency to develop patterns of outreach which move outside the cultural and social boundaries of church life. Much of this ministry could be characterized as being of an incarnational or relational nature. In this incarnational work, which self-consciously looks beyond the fringe of congregations, there is a continuing sensibility that a distance from the church is important. The following are extracts from a recent report from a youthworker in a newly established work which is concerned to reach out to those outside of the church. Under the section 'Problems', the relationship with the church features highly.

Although initiated by the church the youth project is a separate entity. We draw people from the churches, train them and direct them, rather than facilitating the church. This means that, although supported by the churches, we are not owned by them.

None of the clergy are involved in the running of the youth project.

Communicating with a number of different churches in different areas has proved difficult, and has affected the prayer support we receive.

There is no church fellowship which could disciple the young people we are working with in a culturally relevant way.

This brief snapshot of one project in a UK town serves to highlight the issues facing youth ministry in its relationship with the church. In the first instance there is a recognition that to reach out to certain social groups, a new organization is often required. This may be simply a financial consideration but it is also linked to the inflexible structures of many churches. The separate nature of the youthwork leads to innovation and, through innovation, the group finds that it is able to reach those previously untouched by the church. The irony is that once contact with groups outside the reach of the church has been made, it proves almost impossible to bring these young people into the worshipping life of the church. The failure of open youthwork and detached community-based projects to deliver 'bums on pews' has probably been the main reason why many churches have ceased to fund these kinds of projects. A permanent distance from the church has led to the closure of many youthwork projects. Clearly, if we are to see a blossoming of outreach beyond the fringes of the Christian community alongside a necessary distance, there also needs to be a significant closeness to the church.

To tread carefully a close and yet distant line requires a good deal of thought and theological reflection on the part of youth ministers. Resources to promote a sophisticated and informed ecclesiology which deals directly with the concerns and interests of those working amongst young people are essential to the future development of youth ministry in the United Kingdom. If youth ministry is to continue to be effective in working with those who are culturally distant from the church, there is a need for youth ministers, and those in authority over them in the wider church, to come to a shared understanding of issues of closeness and distance. This chapter is written as a tentative first attempt to lay down the issues which need to be worked with if the dialogue is to be successful.

The church in another mode

The history of Christian youthwork in the United Kingdom has been largely defined by the development of youthwork organizations which are separate from the church. The pioneers of Christian youthwork were influenced by William Carey's argument that Christians should use 'means'—that is, voluntary societies—to spread the gospel.[2] As successive generations of Christians have sought to reach out to young people they have created a network of agencies and youthwork organizations. These include the YMCA, founded in 1844 by George Williams; The Children's Special Service Mission (CSSM), started by Joseph Spiers in 1868; and in more recent years, organizations such as Youth For Christ (YFC), which came to Britain following Billy Graham's rallies in the 1950s, and Steve Chalke's Oasis Trust, formed in the 1980s.

Clearly, organizational distance from the church has been an enduring characteristic of youth ministry in Britain for more than 100 years. This parachurch tradition has clearly served the church well; however, in recent times the continued importance of such groups has been called into question. Criticism has firstly arisen within the discipline of mission studies and secondly from the work of Professor Mark Senter.

MISSION STUDIES AND THE PARACHURCH

In mission studies much discussion has taken place as to which structures best serve the church in mission. Ralph Winter's division of the church into 'modalities' (that is, settled congregational groups) and 'sodalities' (that is, the committed apostolic band) appeared to justify the increasing proliferation of parachurch mission agencies.[3] Winter, and later Mellis, argued that the congregation and the mission agency were both 'church'; however, they were fulfilling different functions. The local congregation, or modality, was a welcoming inclusive group with a diversity of concerns: 'The congregation is first and foremost a nurture structure.'[4] The sodality, on the other hand, was a task-oriented, single-purposed group.[5] The key determining factor between these two expressions of church, according to Mellis, is commitment. Within church life: 'Some provision must be made for growing, highly-motivated members to express their deeper commitment. For it is through these people that the church at large becomes dynamic.'[6]

The idea that those involved in the ongoing nurture of Christians are in some way less 'committed' than those who are mainly mission and task-oriented is, at best, hard to sustain as a credible argument and, at worst, insulting and offensive. It is difficult to measure commitment, be it of the nurturing or of the task-based variety. The enduring element, however, in this presentation is the view that new parachurch structures are necessary to the renewal of the church. Mellis examines the history of renewal movements from apostolic times, through early monasticism and the mendicant orders to the development of missionary societies and, more recently, youth organizations such as Operation Mobilization and Youth With A Mission. He sees these groups as each effecting a much needed refreshing of the church. Winter and Mellis, therefore, have argued that the Protestant Church should foster the development of 'orders' committed to mission.[7]

Within missiological circles, support for the sodality argument has come in for much criticism. For Peters, the separate nature of the sodality does damage to the 'body' theology of the church.[8] Perez notes the stormy relationship which often exists between the church and parachurch agencies:

They may first offer their services to complement the work of the church in some particular weakness; then they become competitive for the support from the church in finances, personnel, prayer concern and other areas of common interest; in some cases they become antagonistic by setting up their own programme as of primary importance over and against the programme of the church.[9]

Vinay Samuel and Chris Sugden have likened parachurch agencies to multinational organizations which are preventing the effective spread of the gospel. In many cases this is because the mission agencies choose to bypass the local church and act independently.[10] Having said this, Samuel and Sugden are not rejecting the essential function of 'sodalities' in the economy of mission. They stand with Winter and Mellis in stating that: 'History shows that the chief bearers of mission have always been groups within the church who have come together under the call of God to make mission their chief activity.'[11] The multinational characteristics of the mission agencies have come about because they have been successful over the past thirty years. Far from dismissing sodalities, therefore, Samuel and Sugden advocate that multinational mission agencies need to become subject to 'sodalities' within the Two-Thirds World who are the main source of an effective critique of their work.

In my view there are significant parallels between the discussions taking place within mission studies and the situation of youth ministry in the United Kingdom. In the first instance, it is important to affirm the need for the church to evolve structures which allow for innovation and experimentation. The church needs to allow space for small, creative groups of people to experiment with new forms of youth ministry. In some cases these groups may fail, but in others they may be prophetic for the future evolution of the whole church. To do this they need to establish a certain distance from the church and, for this reason, such distance should be encouraged.

At the same time, however, the discussion within mission studies highlights the extent to which these separate parachurch organizations can themselves become problems to the church as they evolve. It is crucial that in assessing the role of parachurch groups we keep in mind the innovative function of sodalities. The primary reason for the existence of sodalities is that they allow space for new approaches to be generated. In time, however, it is to be expected that the church will begin to adopt the approaches developed by these groups. In the United Kingdom, at present, it is clear that churches are increasingly appointing their own youth ministers who are to a large extent adopting approaches pioneered by parachurch groups such as Scripture Union (SU), Crusaders and Youth For Christ (YFC). The churches, therefore, have assimilated the innovation of the existing parachurch groups. This leaves us with a situation where parachurch and church share a common evangelical subculture and share methods of working with young people. Youthwork, be it done by Crusaders, YFC, SU or a local church, will very often be substantially the same. In this new climate, therefore, parachurch groups which have ceased to be on the cutting edge of ministry are competing for resources with churches to do very similar kinds of work. This leads us directly on to the work of Mark Senter.

THE COMING REVOLUTION IN YOUTH MINISTRY

According to Senter, youthwork in the United States has developed through a series of what he terms revolutions.

Each revolution ushers in a new and fresh approach to ministry amongst young people. Senter begins by noting that most of the established ministries in the United States were started in the 1940s, 1950s or the 1960s. In the late 1980s, he found that the two most influential youth ministries, YFC and Young Life were not simply looking dated and set in their ways, but that they were also attracting declining numbers of young people to their work.[12] The stage is set, therefore, in Senter's view, for a new generation of youth ministers to emerge. As for the existing organizations:

If history is any indicator, both organizations will be around 50 years from now and will have a ministry to a specific clientele. The main stream of youth ministry, however, will be flowing through different channels.[13]

Senter discerns three previous cycles in work amongst young people in the United States: two English movements—the Sunday School and the YMCA—in 1824–75; The Young People's Society for Christian Endeavor and its denominational counterparts in 1881–1925; and Youth For Christ and Young Life in 1935–87. Examining these movements, Senter sees a process which repeats itself:

The cycles of youth ministry did have a predictable shape to them. They started amid a period of rapid social change and soon saw grassroots youth ministries springing up under the hand of the Holy Spirit all across the nation. In time an acknowledged leader emerged in the form of a nationally recognized youth ministry organization, but, though its ministry continued for years, imitators began using the essential strategy without the well focused purpose. After a period of slow stagnation, an event outside of the youth ministry changed the environment and set the stage for the next cycle.[14]

The extent to which Senter's specific argument can be directly applied to the United Kingdom awaits further work; however, the general point—that parachurch agencies go through an evolution—seems to be applicable. The present UK scene is awash with innovation and experimentation. In some cases this is within the parachurch organizations, but more often it is to be seen amongst locally based and often church-linked youthwork projects. What these projects have in common is a willingness to wrestle with issues of culture. Whether the project is focused on new worship or on reaching out to young people beyond the fringe or the church, there is a generic theme which revolves around the way that the gospel and worship arise from youth culture. It is this commonality which affects the style of these new initiatives in youth ministry, and which marks them as being essentially different from the prevailing Christian culture pervading both the evangelical church and the longstanding parachurch organizations.[15]

Those who are on the cutting edge of youth ministry in the United Kingdom are increasingly dealing with questions of culture and worship, and the contextualization of the gospel within a variety of different youth subcultures. It is the argument of this chapter that these endeavours carry within them a certain logic which necessitates a degree of distance and also a requirement for a closeness to the church. In the final part of this chapter, I will set out some preliminary thoughts on the nature of the distance and closeness between youth ministers and the church which best helps the growth of outreach beyond the culture of the church.

The need for distance

To engage in mission is to begin to be concerned with issues, people and so on that are rarely, if ever, on the agenda of the church. In other words, if to engage in incarnational mission is to give yourself wholeheartedly to people outside of the church, it is also to some extent to cut oneself off from the primary interests of the church. Thus, interest in 'fellowship' or the health of the Sunday School, or the latest Christian event or personality, begins to disappear the further one travels into the life and world of the young people. The Christian subculture consequently loses some of its fascination when it is viewed through the eyes of the young people one has got to know. The realization that the latest Christian band, theatre company or speaker will cut little or no ice with the young people one is seeking to reach dampens one's enthusiasm. Moreover, this sense of the relative merits of the Christian subculture produces an inevitable friction given the often exaggerated claims of the Christian subculture to be relevant or in touch with young people. There follows a twofold reaction for the youth minister. First, there is a sense of lostness and separation which comes about as the Christian subculture is seen to exhibit signs of being 'the emperor's suit of clothes'. Second, as this realization begins to sink in, the youth minister starts to question his or her own involvement and nurture within this subculture. The evangelical subculture is resistant to relativizing tendencies. It is, therefore, something of a shock to find that the context within which you yourself found faith and were nurtured will not similarly help the young people you have come to know. The relativizing of the evangelical subculture involves a major paradigm shift on the part of the youth minister. Suddenly what was seen as a universal answer to the problems of the world becomes one approach amongst many others to Christian truth.

Such a paradigm shift within the belief structure and spirituality of the youth minister is often accompanied by a need for a distance from that subculture of the church. This is required for three reasons.

⊙ The realization that the evangelical subculture is one contextualized expression of the gospel amongst others is difficult to grasp from within the subculture. Somehow one needs to distance oneself from the mainstream of evangelical church life in order to imagine something different.

⊙ It is a common experience of youth ministers that as they seek to relativize their own experience of the faith, they come into conflict with church leaders and even their own friends. In part, this will be because many evangelical Christians are threatened by the new ideas and questions raised by the youth minister. It will also be the case, however, that the youth minister will need to rock the boat somewhat to test out his or her own new ideas. Some of this questioning will be unwarranted, and perhaps unfair, but it is an almost inevitable part of the process of creating a distance in order that something new may begin to be imagined.

⊙ There is a clear sense that the people in the local church congregation seem to live in a different cultural and social world from the young people one has got to know. This realization only becomes a reality when looking at the church from the perspective of the outsider. To take on the attitudes and values, and to share in some of the life experiences, of the young people one is seeking to reach is essential to incarnational mission. However, it also inevitably means that one views the evangelical church as being of less significance. Such a perspective brings with it a sense of separation and distance.

Distance and imagination

It is inherent within an incarnational model of youth ministry that new patterns of living out and speaking the good news have to be constructed. The youth minister is self-consciously choosing to enter the world of a particular group of young people. This movement necessarily involves a search for a connection between the context of these young people and the Good News of Christ. This endeavour is far from marginal to the practice of incarnational youth ministry, indeed it is the wish to express Good News which guides and informs everything that the youth minister does. The problem, however, is that patterns for acting out and speaking the Good News hitherto seen by the youth minister will most probably have been formulated within the subculture of the church.

It is an act of imagination which helps the youth minister to begin to formulate a programme of care and, eventually, a verbal expression of the faith which grows from the context of a particular group of young people. In order to see 'the new' it is sometimes necessary to get a little distance from the old. The culture of the church represents a powerful draw on the youth minister. In the first instance, it might be that in order to conceive that something might be different, the youth minister may need to gain a psychological distance. This distancing could be compared to the need of adolescents to separate temporarily from their parents in order that they might gain their own individuality.

The separation required to imagine a different expression of the gospel is also needed for practical reasons. In the first place, a strong link between the organization of the church and the incarnational ministry means that youth ministers are continually drawn back into the programmes of the church. Clergy find it hard to accept that the youth minister does not want to be involved in the latest mission or Bible study programme, and so on. This pressure to be a full and integral part of the church community is endemic to all posts connected with the church.

The church, however, is not always at fault in this context. In some cases, the youth ministers themselves may lack the conviction or the courage to express the faith in new ways. This problem can be particularly acute when it comes to a verbal proclamation of the faith. It is a temptation for the youth minister, who might be more inclined to offer practical care and relationship building, to try to avoid responsibility for the verbal proclamation of the faith. Whilst accepting that such activity is necessary to the process of evangelism, the youthworker may look to traditional church methods and people to fulfil this aspect of the work. A degree of independence and separation from the church reduces these two tendencies whilst encouraging the development of new patterns of expression.

Church planting and youth ministry

An incarnational approach to youth ministry will result in the creation of indigenous faith communities. There is, therefore, a dual 'incarnation' which takes place in youth ministry. In the first instance, the youth minister 'translates' the gospel by actions and words into the context of a particular community and group of young people. This initial expression of the faith, however, will be taken up by the young people themselves. Very soon the ministry becomes focused on the way that Jesus becomes 'real' within the context and lives of these young people. This is a second incarnation, that is when Jesus enters a new subculture and begins to redeem it from within.

When the gospel takes root within one particular group, what begins to emerge is an indigenous faith community. This often small and fragile group could easily be discouraged, colonized or simply merged into the existing church. It is at this point, however, that the youth minister needs to work hard to protect the integrity and independence of this group. Carlos Mesters' description of base communities in Latin America as being like a 'defenseless flower'[16] which might so easily be crushed underfoot would seem to be a very apt description of these groups. Yet paradoxically it is to these vulnerable local indigenous communities that we should look for the renewal of the church.

Closeness to the church

The emergence of groups such as The Nine O'Clock Service in Sheffield and The Late Late Service in Glasgow has served to inspire youthworkers in the United Kingdom to seek to see new forms of worship develop out of work amongst young people. An incarnational theology of youth ministry, whilst advocating a 'distance' from the local congregation, will see as the result of its work the emergence of new congregations. In one sense it is in this last stage that one sees the work begin to come full circle. Incarnational ministry is a journey which at first takes one into a wilderness beyond the safety of accepted church life, but in time there is a sense of returning to a form of church which is, at one and the same time, familiar and yet also different.

Whilst the youth minister may need to find a distance from the culture of the local congregation and, in some cases, a freedom from control by the institution, there is also a sense in which those seeking to incarnate the gospel beyond the boundaries of the church never cease to be the church. This, it would seem, is the main conclusion one can draw from the discussions within mission studies. Having said this, there are fundamental reasons why youth ministers, whilst requiring a distance from the church, also need to develop strategies for keeping in contact and in fellowship with local congregations.

LOCAL FAITH COMMUNITIES NEED THE CHURCH

I have argued at length elsewhere that whilst there is a need for young people to begin to evolve their own expressions of the faith, they also need to be linked with well-established churches. This is important, first, because the institutional nature of the church offers a stability and a freedom which paradoxically allows the new communities to experiment and be radical. Sectarian groups in contrast have a poor history in this regard.[17] A close link with an institutional church also offers a tradition for the young people to experiment with in worship. This is done through a kind of symbolic play as the tradition of the church is combined in different ways with aspects of youth culture.[18]

It is essential that the new and fragile faith community is welcomed and supported by the institutional church. In the first instance, this might simply be willingness on the part of ministers to recognize the new group as a legitimate expression of the faith. It might be that the institutional church is able to offer a home within their building. Such a pattern is becoming well accepted within the Anglican Church. These associations are often experimental in nature, but it is important that clergy and lay people within the church learn to welcome young people who are building faith communities.

There is also a sense in which the institutional church needs to grant the new faith communities their 'churchness'. In the Anglican Church the key element in this is willingness for the new faith communities to be accepted fully into the sacramental life of the church. The role of the priest in the Anglican Church is central to the legitimization that the church may offer to young people.[19] The new faith community needs the institutional church to welcome it as a real and genuine expression of the faith. This is a gift of God's grace which only the church can give to the group.

It is a fact that the faith communities need the institutional church, which means that youth ministers have a responsibility to keep in close contact with local churches.

THE NEED TO EDUCATE THE CHURCH

If local clergy and lay people are to welcome young people who are forming faith communities, there is a responsibility for youth ministers to educate and inform the local church. Given the need for distance from the church it is a tough assignment to be told also to keep in close contact with the church. This, however, is an essential role for youth ministers. At every point, through newsletters and through informal contact, church people need to be kept in touch with the work. Given the nature of the paradigm shift required on the part of youth ministers as they work outside the subculture of the church, it is to be expected that considerable sensitivity and patience is necessary as the local church slowly learns about what is developing in the work with young people.

My own experience in this regard is that there is very little substitute for informal contact between local church people and young people. It is important to try to take key clergy and lay people on 'exposure visits' to meet with young people. We have also encouraged young people to share their stories with local church people. However, in most cases we have avoided getting young people into a church service to do this. It is best to find a venue where the young people feel comfortable and unthreatened for such sharing to take place.

THE NEED FOR SUPPORT

The youth minister needs the prayer support and fellowship of other Christians. Incarnational ministry is demanding and should never be undertaken alone. Once again, given the need for distance from the culture of the church, there is also a considerable period when the youth minister will need a sensitive and encouraging group of people to turn to for support. Youth ministers, as part of engaging incarnationally in a new social and cultural context, will need to evolve a spirituality which will sustain them as they move into the unknown and leave behind the safety of the church subculture. It is possible to move entirely outside the church circle, but to do so is to court spiritual disenchantment. Youth ministers, therefore, need to move in and out of church life, eventually finding an accommodation and acceptance of the difference between their calling and the calling of those they need to have fellowship with.

Support, however, will often mean a financial relationship between the youth minister and local Christians. This financial relationship will necessitate a degree of accountability. Once again, the need for clear understanding of what is involved in incarnational ministry and sensitive management on the part of those responsible for the correct use of funds are important. Regular communication and adequate supervision are essential ingredients. Where a youth minister is employed by a management group, there is obviously a need for a shared vision. However, it should be recognized that this group will need to learn and grow as the ministry itself evolves. In this sense, even where there is a financial and organizational distance from the church there is a vital connection with the body of Christ which is worked out through the management committee.

Conclusion

Youth ministry in the United Kingdom has traditionally been supported through parachurch structures. In this sense, a certain 'distance from the church' has been a regular and normal part of church life. The argument for parachurch structures, however, revolves around the means by which the church renews itself by spawning innovative and experimental communities of mission. Given this fact, there is some weight in the arguments of Senter and mission theologians that such groups are temporary and cyclical. Organizational distance from the church is, therefore, only a function of the need to reach beyond the culture of the church. When innovative outreach ceases to take place, or when the church assimilates the new methods, the parachurch group has little reason to exist other than to maintain itself.

Amongst the new generation of youth ministers the distance sought from the church has been less organizational and structural than it has been cultural. Distance, in this sense, is created by the need to create a contextual theology based in particular youth subcultures. To contextualize the faith has necessitated a distance from the subcultural norms of the evangelical church. Much of this work is grass roots based, but it has generally maintained relationships with local churches and congregations. In this sense it has been characterized by both distance and closeness. As time goes on growth in outreach to the unchurched will depend on the ability of the church and youth ministers to understand the dynamic between innovative youth ministry and the church.

NOTES

1. Robert Warren, *Being Human, Being Church*, Harper Collins, 1995; Mike Hill, *Reaching the Unchurched*, Alpha, 1994.

2. Perez in Bruce Nicholls (ed) *The Church God's Agent for Change*, WEF/Paternoster, 1986, p. 207.

3. Ralph Winter, 'The Two Structures of God's Redemptive Mission', *Missiology*, January 1974.

4. Charles J. Mellis, *Committed Communities*, The William Carey Library 1983, p. 4.

5. Eddie Gibbs, *I Believe in Church Growth*, Hodder and Stoughton, 1981, p. 345.

6. Mellis, *Committed Communities*, p. 5.

7. Perez in Nicholls, *The Church*, p. 204.

8. Perez in Nicholls, *The Church*, p. 204.

9. Perez in Nicholls, *The Church*, p. 211.

10. Vinay Samuel and Chris Sugden, *Mission Agencies as Multinationals*, International Review of Mission, 1983, p. 152.

11. Samuel and Sugden, *Missions Agencies*, p. 154.

12. Mark Senter III, *The Coming Revolution in Youth Ministry*, 1992, p. 22.

13. Senter, *The Coming Revolution*, p. 23.

14. Senter, *The Coming Revolution*, p. 70.

15. For more on this see Ward 'The Case for Contextualised Theology of Youth Sub-Cultures' in Ward and Lim, *Adolescence, Youth Ministry and World Mission*, Paternoster, 1995.

16. Carlos Mesters, *Defenseless Flower*, Orbis, 1989.

17. Pete Ward, *Youth Culture and the Gospel*, Harper Collins, 1992, pp. 171–182.

18. Pete Ward, *Worship and Youth Culture*, Harper Collins, 1993, pp. 51–57.

19. See Ward, *Worship and Youth Culture*, p. 86–89.

4

Paradigms in the contemporary church that reflect generational values

STEVE GERALI

Process of contextualization

Through the centuries the church has wrestled with its ability to contextualize the gospel to various cultures. There have been countless hours of debate over the process of contextualization. Many have seen the contextualization of the gospel to be 'a way to develop authentic and relevant responses to the Christian message that would lead to significant and beneficial changes among individuals and groups as well as to the confirmation of the worth and value of the message' (Lazenby, 1990). Lazenby continues to advance the view that those holding to this theory must contemplate a problem. The problem arises with the emphasis put on the word 'change', when that which is to change is never defined. Often the 'change' that occurs is cultural in that a dominant culture superimposes a cultural Christianity on a second culture. The second culture does not contextualize the gospel, rather it assimilates or conforms to the values of the dominant culture. This became evident when the gospel was taken into Two Thirds World countries. Missionaries propagated a Western form of Christianity. Biblical principles were interpreted and presented in the light of Western culture forms, not the cultural forms of those Two-Thirds World countries. Lazenby illustrates this, saying:

Since these principles are inextricably connected to the thought-forms and values of the Western culture, the African church will of necessity only reflect a Western form of Christianity. If there is to be a genuine contextualization, the Western missionary and his or her 'biblical principles' need to change in addition to the African and his or her culture... To accomplish this task, contextualization as a concept can be described more specifically as a continuing process of change whereby different contexts are joined or woven together in such a way that a coherence is established among them. This implies that all the contexts involved must undergo some degree of change. The goal in this kind of contextualization is not conformity of one context with another but coherence among the various contexts. The end result is not the elimination of differences among the contexts but the joining together of those differences to establish a coherent framework for further contextualization. (Lazenby, 1990, p. 3; emphasis added).

This is threatening to the church because the church has tended to blur the line between biblical principle and its cultural interpretation of biblical principle, thus making its cultural values synonymous with biblical principle. The contemporary church movement was born out of this form of contextualization. It largely challenged the values, norms and practices of the traditional church; took from the traditional church that which reached a new generation of individuals; and reshaped the context by allowing the values of the new generation to form the new context of the gospel. In other words, the contemporary church reaches a generation of baby-boomers because it accurately contextualizes the gospel to that generation. This shift was met with resistance by the traditional church labelling the coherence of contexts as 'compromise' (Tapia, 1994). Today many churches still struggle with this perceived 'compromise' and are attempting to buy into the contemporary church movement; thus putting some churches behind the times and keeping the contemporary church movement a relatively new phenomenon.

What mainline contemporary churches fail to see is that they have become baby-boomer value driven. That which is a phenomenon to the baby-boomer (having grown up in traditional churches) is viewed as traditional to the succeeding generation of baby-busters, or 'Generation Xers', who were born into the contemporary church. The contemporary church now sits in the seat of the traditional church and forgets its heritage and the process of contextualization that shaped its success. Those baby-boomer values which drive the contemporary church growth movement have become sacred; the line between biblical principle and the cultural interpretation of biblical principle has become blurred. The contemporary church, having been built and enmeshed in the generational values of the baby-boomer, is alienating a generation of adolescents (Generation Xers) who are coming of age.

George Barna (1992) states that the church needs to change or it will lose the baby-buster generation. Barna says, 'In terms of evangelism, we have a generation coming up that doesn't speak the same language, doesn't go to the same places, doesn't have the same needs, and isn't looking to Christianity to answer their spiritual concerns... we either change or we lose them.' This basic belief is even starting to penetrate the advertising industry. Peter Kim, US Director for Strategic Planning at J. Walter Thompson North America, noted that baby-boomers will be making a big mistake if they assume that the baby-buster is just like them when they (the boomers) were that age. Kim says: 'Most marketers today are boomers and are much more likely to impose their values on this generation, to the point where busters are invisible' (as cited in Zinn, 1992). Russell (1993) notes that baby-boomers dominate the demographic landscape and that US culture bends to their will, 'reflecting their prejudices and passions'. It would be foolish for one to assume that the church has escaped this domination. Before we can determine what the specific values for each of these generations are, we must have a basic understanding of who these people are.

Boomer and buster generations

Baby-boomers are people who were born in the 1940s and 1950s, and came of age in the 1960s and 1970s. They make up the largest generation in the history of the United States (Strauss and Howe, 1991; Howe and Strauss, 1992, 1993). They have cornered the market on industry and commerce, having been the first generation to have free access to higher education (Senter, 1992; Russell, 1993). They came of age in an era where they experienced the acceptance of adolescence as a distinct age stage; the birth of rock and roll; the sexual revolution; the civil rights movement; an experimental drug culture; the space and nuclear arms races; the Vietnam War; the assassination of a US president; and Woodstock. All this served to develop the 'anti-establishment' attitude that typified this generation.

Boomers were told that they could be anything and could accomplish anything, which gave rise to the 'human potential movement' (Strauss and Howe, 1991), propagating total self-sufficiency, rugged individualism and (in some cases) the deification of the individual (Russell, 1993). Susan Hayward, senior vice-president of Yankelovich Partners Inc., a marketing firm said, 'Boomers were told as kids, "You're wonderful, you're the centre of the universe", and boomers will feel that way until they are 90' (as cited in Zinn, 1992). Hayward, when describing the buster, noted that everything from a collapsing economy to the absence of a mother at home robbed the buster of the same optimism. 'Upward-mobility', 'climbing the corporate ladder' and 'rising to leadership' have become common value phrases to the boomer. Boomers have occupied, and are continuing to occupy, seats of power and leadership on a national and international scale, not only in government but also in the church. It would be strategic to note that these are the people who are shaping the vision, strategies and direction of the church and the church growth movement.

Baby-busters (also known as Generation Xers, thirteenth gen., slackers, twenty-somethings and so on) are people who were born in the 1960s and 1970s. They are coming of age in the 1980s and 1990s. This generation is the second largest generation of children to be born in the United States (Strauss and Howe, 1991; Tapia, 1994; Dunn, 1993; Howe and Strauss, 1992, 1993). This generation is the first generation that sees themselves as being less affluent than their parents (Howe and Strauss, 1993).

The Generation Xers are the first generation of latchkey children. They are the products of dual-income families and/or single parent families (more than 50 per cent have grown up in homes where parents are divorced, separated or remarried with other children). This generation was raised having to fend for themselves, often before their readiness. Because of this, they are consumer-aware, having to be the primary shopper for groceries and household products. This abandonment and premature responsibility have aided in the growth of the angst that this generation feels.

Whereas the boomer was classified as the first media generation, the media blitz was perfected on the Generation Xer who is the cable (MTV) generation. More is at their fingertips. They have never known life without microwaves, cable networks, compact discs, electronic games, computer-generated everything, home video entertainment and the advent of virtual reality.

Developmentally, this population of late adolescents must complete the task known as 'intimacy versus isolation' (Erikson, 1968). This is the developmental stage, where intimate relationships formulate and life friendships take root. Every generation must pass through this developmental stage, but this generation has rarely experienced intimacy, and has greater needs and values with regard to relationships. Schultz *et al* (1991) note that MTV seeks to generate 'intimacy without relationship' for a generation whose primary caretaker was a television. Zinn (1992) states that 'grunge, anger, cultural dislocation and a secret yearning to belong... add up to a daunting cultural anthropology that marketers have to confront if they want to reach the twenty-somethings'.

Generation Xers are anti-boomer. They do not want to be like the boomer nor do they embrace boomer values and culture. They see themselves as an alternative nation with alternative music representative of alternative lifestyles. They have become content with living on less; desire more intimate relationships; are more embracing of diversity in race and gender; are more accommodating of social need; and their individual identity is not based on what they accomplish, but rather on who they are. Their definition of success is relational fulfilment as opposed to financial gain.

When you place these two generations side by side, it is not difficult to see the difference in generational values. Examination of the generational values and the paradigms that grow out of them would consume volumes, yet one must look at some of the more dominant boomer values that have shaped the contemporary church. While this list is not exhaustive, the following values have become a driving force in the contemporary church growth movement. As they are examined, the process of contextualization should be broached, begging the question as to whether or not the contemporary church will reach the Generation Xers.

Examination of generational values

The first major generational value is what each generation holds to be 'culturally relevant'. To the baby-boomer, cultural relevance means 'trendy'. They want timely drama, contemporary light-rock music, and a cadre of multi-media audio and visual experiences. In the contemporary church, the church organ was replaced by a band, liturgy was replaced with media and icons were removed to give a worship centre the look of a theatre. Ostling (1993) points out that baby-boomers attend churches where:

Jeans are as welcomed as suits and ties; theater seats replace pews. Instead of using hymnbooks, congregations sing lively, if saccharine, choruses with words projected on a screen. Worship may include skits, audience participation or applause (Ostling, 1993, p. 47).

The baby-boomer realizes that these worship trends can be, and are, costly. They are willing to pay the price because they reach their generation. That price is not often just financial but comes in the form of criticism. Many of an older traditional generation still argue the evils of using pop culture in the church. They feel that the church must distance itself from appearing like the world. Leaders of the contemporary church suffer the scars of this battle and still deal with its residual effect. Yet they see that the entertainment approach to ministry reaches boomers. Avery Dulles, a Catholic theologian, concludes that just about everything in the United States, including religion, 'succeeds to the extent that it can arouse interest and provide entertainment' (cited in Ostling,

1993). Most North American values are shaped and influenced by the prejudices and passions of the baby-boomer. Boomers seek a polished, entertaining approach to everything. This polished, somewhat flawless presentation of products, has become synonymous with those products being seen as 'excellent' in the mind of the boomer. The Generation Xers, on the other hand, have never faced the issues of the evils of pop culture in worship settings. Thus they find the contemporary art favoured by the boomers to be a watered-down, and stagnant, art form. Tapia (1994) states, 'To the buster crowd, Christian music often feels old-fashioned or, if contemporary, not up to the highest standards.' Generation Xers want worship to be passionate and honest. They are more attracted to a coffee-house concept of worship than to the theatre approach. Generation Xers view the boomers' buy-in to trendy approaches as superficial. The entertainment approach that reaches boomers is considered to be a slick packaging of the Christian experience to the buster.

Generation Xers see this slick packaging as deceptive. They are very consumer aware. Where boomers see Generation Xers as non-committed, Generation Xers boast that they are cautious, wanting to see authenticity (Tapia, 1994; Howe and Strauss, 1993; Mahedy and Bernardi, 1994; Giles, 1994). They do not view the contemporary church as authentic, so they are reluctant to commit to its attractive packaging. Generation Xers have been burned by slick packaging and broken promises. They are irresolute to trust anything that appears to be a gimmick to them. They want the bottom line without all the hype, glamour and polish.

Some 96 per cent of the baby-boomer population in North America were raised in a religious tradition, but 58 per cent abandoned it as young adults (Roof, 1993). Many are returning to church out of responsibility to the rearing of their children and/or personal or career crises facilitated out of mid-life (Ostling, 1993). These returnees still have a bitter taste in their mouths about the traditions of religious institutions. The church growth experts have sensed this and have not only changed the format of the worship experience, but also the facility. Icons have become a thing of the past and church buildings are more 'functional', taking on the look of a corporate headquarters, mall or arts centre. While this reaches the boomer, Generation Xers see it as corporate American (which they detest), and feel misled because there is no physical evidence that identifies the community or religious tenets of the church. Generation Xers are not threatened by icons or symbols; as a matter of fact, they embrace them. The rock star Prince has changed his name and existence to be represented by a symbol. It has even become fashionable among busters to have symbols tattooed on their bodies. Having grown up in a post-modern world, Generation Xers are seeking a more mystical religious experience as opposed to a rational, didactic religion. Icons and symbols become an attraction for the Generation Xer.

Another generational difference grows out of each generation's view of itself. As was stated earlier, baby-boomers were raised in an optimistic setting where they learned to be somewhat invincible, self-sufficient and individualistic. This value permeates so much of what a baby-boomer is and does that the individual may even be oblivious to it. As a result of this, boomers tend to draw their identity from what they do. Achievement becomes the hallmark of the boomer's existence. Light (1988) notes that the first point on the baby-boomer agenda is the search for personal and economic opportunity. Callahan (1983), a church growth expert, notes that the mark of strong leadership in the church is determined by how much the congregation achieves. He stresses the point that accomplishments supersede activities.

A common boomer anthem heralds: 'He who dies with the most toys wins.' This philosophy drives the boomer to build empires in business, politics, recreation and religion. Never before have we seen church growth become such a drive of the religious community. This focus views growth of the kingdom of God or body of Christ as being synonymous with the proportional growth of the local church body. Thus success is tangible and measurable. Satelliting churches is not a strategic part of the church growth movement. Pastors (many of whom are boomers) view the success of their ministry in how large the local church can become. Church growth experts do not see a unity of local churches, rather they propose the view of building a single congregation to monumental size. Russell (1993) notes that to boomers 'competition rather than cooperation is the key to success, and this fosters individualism'. Carl George (1991) proposes the metachurch strategy. George says:

> *The term meta-church... signifies both a change of mind about how ministry is to be done and a change of form in the infrastructure of the church. Meta- and 'huge' don't necessarily go together. Meta-church principles lead to a recognizable organizational framework, a social architecture without inherent expansion limits. If implemented properly, very large growth can result. But any size church can begin the transformation into a Meta-church (George, 1991, p. 57).*

George states that 'huge' and 'meta-' do not necessarily go together but he identifies that large growth is the result and purpose of the metachurch strategy. George (1990), in his Meta-Church Cluster Consultation Seminars, does identify a metachurch as being beyond huge (more than 10,0000 attendees), and as being larger and smaller than ever (smaller, because of the small group clusters). Baby-boomers and baby-boomer pastors share these values. Metachurch is cohesive with the values of the boomer generation and it attracts boomers.

Generation Xers have an entirely different set of values. They do not idealize individualism (Howe and Strauss, 1993), nor do they embrace a philosophy that demands bigger to be better or more effective. Big churches with big programmes, big budgets, big facilities and so on become a repellent to the Generation Xer. 'Down-sizing' is not a dirty word to the Generation Xer but, rather, it means that something will be more manageable, relational or genuine. 'Smaller' is seen as good, thus there is no desire or need to build empires or accomplish great feats because the Generation Xers' identity is not rooted in their work. Generation Xers tend to herald the anthem 'he who dies with the most toys still dies'. They view their jobs as a means of support not a means of identity. Often overqualified and underemployed they have what Doug Coupland (1991) labels 'Mc-Jobs' or mundane and marginally challenging work that provides a means of support. Howe and Strauss (1993) say:

They [Generation Xers] work as hard as they need to—but when the work is over, it is over. They're not workaholics and don't labor needlessly on weekends (like boomers) for the perverse joy of it. Possessed of a purely instrumental view of employment, they can distance themselves from corporate cultures and can relax without guilt when the 'job' is done. (Howe and Strauss, 1993, p. 110).

This distancing from corporate culture is exactly what they do when they encounter the metachurch. The internal structure and workings of the church growth church resembles a corporation. Church growth experts devise strategies that include everything from corporate management skills to church marketing techniques. Demographic studies, target audiences and direct mailings become a focus of the contemporary church. Stephen Long of Duke University Divinity School observes that while using marketing techniques is not wrong as a strategy to reach boomers, it is beginning to appear that marketing techniques are using the church (cited in Ostling, 1993).

At this point it is important to note that the boomer views church growth as the mandate of the great commission of Christ (Matthew 28:18–20) (see Wagner, 1984). Through their cultural grid, boomers strategize ways to reach the world (other boomers) thus fulfilling the mandate of the great commission. The Generation Xers see things very differently. They are more concerned with long-term relationships, not corporate buy-in. They are less cause-driven and tend to feel more for the underdog. To the Generation Xers, the boomers' interpretation of the great commission is just another self-inflating generational cause. Boomers have argued that Generation Xers are ignoring Christ's mandate, while Generation Xers see boomers as 'driven, isolated individuals who miss the concept of embracing the body of Christ' (Tapia, 1994).

Another generational value difference that has been alluded to is the boomers' value of corporation versus the Generation Xers' value of community. Because baby-boomers value individualism, they will see relationships differently from Generation Xers. Boomers are a transient, upwardly mobile, individualistic generation. They need less in relationships because they find fulfilment in other things. Their relationships have design and function. Russell (1993) observes that boomers favour their personal needs over community needs and they tend to make commitments for personal gain rather than for moral reasons. Light (1988) also resonates that boomers are more committed to self than they are to community.

Functional relationships are the agenda of the boomer. With regard to the church, they see small groups as being the vehicle to grow a church and evangelize a community. Yet these small groups are transient. The metachurch theory (George, 1990, 1991) proposes that churches grow by reproducing small relational groups. A by-product of this group is to deliver care, among other things, to its members. The chief function of this small group is to enable the individuals to grow, so that they in turn will fill an empty chair in the group, thus enabling the group to grow. When a group reaches a designated size, they will reproduce by splitting into two smaller groups and start the growth process once again. This process should happen often and should not take longer than one or two years. It illustrates the boomer value for functional transient relationships. Small group theorists may argue that closed groups (as opposed to reproducing groups) die, but there is no substantial, quantifiable research that validates this assumption. It would be easy to understand that to the baby-boomer closed groups die because that type of group doesn't harmonize with boomer values. Sociological perspectives would support that closed groups did in fact work for the 'silent generation', the generation that preceded the boomer generation and is labelled the 'establishment' by boomers (Strauss and Howe, 1991).

This programming of relationships in church growth strategies is even reflected by Callahan (1983). He identifies the 'Callahan's principle of visitation'. This principle holds that pastors should spend one hour in visitation with parishioners, unchurched, newcomers, and so on, per week for every minute that they preach on any given Sunday morning. Callahan (1983) states:

It is important to realize that the purpose of these visits with unchurched families is not to get them into the church. I would describe these as mission visits where the focus is on sharing effecting help and resources with unchurched persons as they seek to live meaningfully and fully in everyday life. Indeed the focus is on being the church with them where they are rather than on seeking to get them to come to church on Sunday mornings (Callahan, 1983, p. 15).

Callahan is enmeshed in the boomer corporate value regarding relationship because earlier he notes that the visitation principle will 'be helpful toward the development of an effective and successful church' and that 'it invites the pastor to think through those strategic priorities that will best advance the church toward becoming increasingly effective and successful' (Callahan, 1983, p. 12). Later, Callahan gives five steps in a visit (which include stating the direction, content, limits and objectives of the visit) and ten foundational principles of the art of effecting visitation. Boomers would largely identify with this because it reflects their values. This agenda would alienate Generation Xers.

Generation Xers value community over corporation, and 'community' to them means something different than it does to the boomer. They are not as transient as the boomer. The rise in American Community Colleges is a tribute to the permanency of the Generation Xer. Generation Xers long for relationships that are authentic, meaningful, spontaneously generated and life-long. They have known little of this in their life, being the product of divorced homes and having become 'throw-away' kids. They not only long for this, but they seek it at all costs, therefore they value it above all other things. Their measure of success and fulfilment lies in the quality of their relationships. Howe and Strauss (1993) accurately capture the essence of this Generation Xer value:

Friends and family matter enormously. She gets along well with her parents; she even likes their music. She despises nothing more than divorce and cruelty to children, having known too much of that herself. She celebrates unconditional love, because she hasn't known enough of it herself. She can smile readily at strangers if necessary for her job, but she reserves genuine emotion for those close to her. Beyond family, her civic virtue is intensely private. Saving the world matters less than feeding one meal to one hungry child. (Howe and Strauss, 1993, p. 31).

Generation Xers do not want small groups that split and reproduce; they want intimate relationships and that takes time. They don't value being in a relationship for a cause such as growing a big church; they desire to care and be cared for. They also seek multi-generational relationships. They have desires to be in a community that they see as permanent, continually providing guidance, nurture, care and so on; reflecting the attributes of an extended family that they never had. Generation Xers' relationships will even cross ethnic and racial barriers. They are more embracing of the equality of races, ethnic groups and gender than any other generation that preceded them (Howe and Strauss, 1993; Liu, 1994; Rushkoff, 1994; Zinn, 1992; Giles, 1994). They don't even have any taboos about interracial dating and marriage (Liu, 1994; Howe and Strauss, 1993). To the Generation Xer, community is not rooted in cause, it is rooted in long-term unconditional relationships.

Another reflection of the boomers' value of corporation over community is their view of the senior pastor. The contemporary church's efforts take on a corporate business flavour with the senior pastor as the CEO (Chief Executive Officer). When a church is growing, having the goal of being a metachurch (10,000-plus attendees) the senior pastor can be nothing less than a CEO. He must manage and oversee many managers who in turn may have direct contact with people. Metachurch (George, 1990, 1991) describes this model in great detail with various overseers and leaders. In many ways, this model resembles the quasi-corporate pyramid effect that typifies Am-Way, Shackley and the Mary Kay Cosmetic Corporations, among others. Ostling (1993) notes that boomer pastors speak of being 'customer oriented' and that they attend seminars to become 'church growth' experts. A CEO is not a negative role to a boomer. Most CEOs are boomers who have climbed the corporate ladder. Embracing the role of a pastor as a CEO aligns with boomer values. This view alienates Generation Xers in that they do not trust organizational heads. Tapia (1994) states that 'having grown up amidst headlines about fallen tele-evangelists and crooked politicians, Generation Xers' trust in authority figures is low, and cynicism of anything organized, like the church and politics, is high'.

Generation Xers are spiritually sensitive and desirous of a relationship with God. Doug Coupland (1994), the Canadian-born X-generation spokesperson, in his book *Life After God*, concedes his hopelessness and desperateness without God. He speaks for a generation that longs to have a relationship with a God who will not let them be alone; give them hope and meaning to life; and love them unconditionally. Coupland (1994) says, 'My secret is that I need God.' The Generation Xers are poised to be the recipients of a great moving of God's Spirit. They are much more spiritually sensitive, experience-oriented, and have a greater need for supernatural intervention and solutions in their lives and problems. Throughout history, major revivals like the 'Great Awakening' have been facilitated through a generation of late adolescent (eighteen to twenty-eight years of age) recipients. Besides having this population as its recipients, other common factors—such as an opposition to generational values, a large, dominant, middle-class society, social unrest and financial crisis—have aided in facilitating these major spiritual awakenings (Senter, 1992; Schultz, *et al*, 1991). Many of these pieces are positioned with the X-generation (not to mention the generation that follows). Unless true contextualization takes place, the contemporary church will not be in a place to minister to the spiritual needs of the X-generation. Until that time, the generational values of the baby-boomer, as reflected and embraced by the contemporary church, will alienate a generation of adolescents coming of age and will continue to create what Howe and Strauss (1992, 1993) define as the 'new generation gap'.

BIBLIOGRAPHY

Barna, George, *The Invisible Generation*, The Barna Research Group, Ltd, 1992.

Callahan, K., *Twelve Keys to an Effective Church: Strategic Planning for Mission*, San Francisco: Harper and Row Publishers, 1983.

Cohen, Michael, *The Twenty-something American Dream: A Cross-Country Quest for a Generation*, New York: Dutton Books, 1993.

Coupland, Douglas, *Generation X*, New York: St Martin's Press, 1991.

Coupland, Douglas, *Life After God*, New York: Pocket Books, 1994.

Dunn, William, *The Baby Bust: A Generation Comes of Age*, Ithaca, NY: American Demographics, Inc., 1993.

Erikson, Eric, *Identity: Youth and Crisis*, New York: Norton, 1968.

George, Carl, *Meta-church Cluster Consultation Notebook*, seminar sponsored by Charles E. Fuller Institute of Evangelism and Church Growth in Buena Park, CA; 8–10 May 1990.

George, Carl, *Prepare Your Church for the Future*, Grand Rapids, MI: Fleming H. Revell, 1991.

Giles, Jeff, 'Generalizations X', *Newsweek*, June 1994, pp. 62–72.

Howe, N. and Strauss, W., 'The New Generation Gap', *Atlantic*, Volume 4 (December 1992), pp. 67–93.

Howe, N. and Strauss, W., *13th Gen.: Abort, Retry, Ignore, Fail?*, New York: Vintage Books, 1993.

Lazenby, Henry, *God, Change and Chaos: The Contextualization of Religion and Society*, (unpublished manuscript), 1990.

Light, Paul, *Baby Boomers*, New York: W.W. Norton and Co., 1988.

Liu, Eric (ed.), *Next: Young American Writers on the New Generation*, New York: W.W. Norton and Co., 1994.

Luce, Ron, 'How We Can Reach Generation X', *Charisma*, September 1994, pp. 20–27.

Mahedy, W. and Bernardi, J., *A Generation Alone: Xers Making a Place in the World*, Downers Grove, IL: InterVarsity Press, 1994.

Ostling, Richard, 'The Church Search', *Time*, April 1993, pp. 44–49.

Roof, W. C., *A Generation of Seekers: The Spiritual Journeys of the Baby Boom Generation*, San Francisco: Harper Collins Publishers, 1993.

Rushkoff, Douglas, *The GenX Reader*, New York: Ballantine Books, 1994.

Russell, Cheryl, *The Master Trend: How the Baby Boom Generation is Remaking America*, New York: Plenun Press, 1993.

Schultz, Q., Anker, R., Bratt, J., Romanowski, W., Worst, J. and Zuidervaart, L., *Dancing in the Dark: Youth, Popular Culture and the Electronic Media*, Grand Rapids, MI: Eerdmans Publishing Co., 1991.

Sciacca, Fran, *Generation at Risk*, Minneapolis, MN: World Wide Publications, 1990.

Senter, Mark, *The Coming Revolution in Youth Ministry and Its Radical Impact on the Church*, Chicago: Victor Books, 1992.

Strauss, W. and Howe, N., *Generations: The History of America's Future: 1584 to 2069*, New York: William Morrow and Co., 1991.

Tapia, A., 'Reaching the First Post-Christian Generation', *Christianity Today*, September 1994, pp. 18–23.

Tillapaugh, F., *Unleashing the Church: Getting People out of the Fortress and into Ministry*, Ventura, CA: Regal Books, 1982.

Todd, E., *The Explanation of Ideology: Family Structures and Social Systems*, Oxford: Basil Blackwell, 1985.

Todd, E., *The Causes of Progress: Culture, Authority and Change*, Oxford: Basil Blackwell, 1987.

Wagner, C. Peter, *Leading Your Church to Growth*, Ventura, CA: Regal Books, 1984.

Zinn, Laura, 'Move Over Boomers the Busters are Here—and They're Angry', *Business Week*, December 1992, pp. 74–80.

5

Multicultural challenges facing youth ministry

PAUL BORTHWICK

Introduction

We live in a multicultural, international, ever-shrinking world. The interdependencies of global economies, television by satellite and electronic communications have created the 'global village' that McLuhan predicted back in the 1960s. But the ethnic 'jihads' we see in the former Yugoslavia, Rwanda and elsewhere remind us that our world is far from some sort of cohesive unit.

In this world, we seek to proclaim the gospel, but the world we enter is not the world of a few generations ago. In 1800, 86 per cent of those who called themselves Christian were white; by the year 2000, this number will drop to 39 per cent.[1] Christianity has become a non-Western religion. Somewhere between 1980 and 1982 a dramatic change occurred: for the first time since the earliest days of Christianity, the centre of gravity of Christianity shifted from the western hemisphere to the Eastern hemisphere, and from the Northern hemisphere to the Southern.[2] According to Bryant Myers: 'The centre of gravity of the Christian church has moved to the Two-Thirds World where over 50 per cent of today's Christians, and 70 per cent of today's evangelicals, live.'[3]

To this ever-shrinking, interdependent world we come to address the multicultural challenges facing us in youth ministry. We come fully aware of how this multicultural reality confronts us. Refugees, mass immigration, ethnic changes in our countries and our cities, and the shrinking influence of Western culture all alert us to the fact that reaching out to youth requires multicultural sensitivity and wisdom. In the words of Mark Senter, 'The day of the monolithic society for people fifteen years old and younger is a thing of the past. Perhaps it never existed. The new paradigm of youth and children's ministry must be prepared to deal with the pluralism of the new generation.'[4]

To stir our thinking, I want to begin by reminding us all of the global and eternal significance of youth ministry—so that our visions can be expanded to call on God for the wisdom we will need to address the gospel to the youth of this diverse and awesome world.

GLOBAL SIGNIFICANCE

If we raise our eyes up to see beyond our own ministries and our own cultures, we will realize the global significance of youth ministry. Reaching adolescents for Christ is not just a Western phenomena, nor is it a white, middle-class phenomena. *Youth ministry is a global reality*, a challenge bigger than anyone could have imagined back in the era when what we now see as traditional youth ministry laid its foundations.[5]

This global significance can be illustrated both subjectively and objectively. Subjectively, I could tell you about Jos Holtzhausen in Namibia and Angola or John Sagherian in Beirut, and their ministries with Youth for Christ International; Jone Kata and his desire to train youthworkers in Fiji; Emmanuel Oladipo and his global vision for the ministry of Scripture Union with youth and children; and Estuardo Lopez in Ecuador and the youth he has mobilized in the cause of literacy for children.

The NEXUS programme of Young Life, the 'youth' desk of the World Council of Churches, the Youth Commission of the World Evangelical Fellowship, the student ministry of Campus Crusade or the International Fellowship of Evangelical Students, Youth With a Mission, and many others all serve to illustrate one thing: the world is young, and the ministry of the church means dedicating ourselves to multifaceted ministry with the world's youth and children.

But our subjective involvement is built on objective facts. The sheer volume of young people in our world calls us to stand up and take notice of youth ministry as a cross-cultural, global challenge:

⊙ By the year 2000, more than half of our world will be under the age of twenty-five.[6]

⊙ Presently, about one-third of the world (1.8 billion people) is under the age of fifteen, with 85 per cent of these in the Two-Thirds World (Africa, Asia and Latin America).[7]

⊙ In the Two-Thirds World some countries already have more than 50 per cent of their populations under the age of fifteen.[8]

⊙ While those in the Western countries are 'greying' and youth ministry as a priority may be called into question, the non-Western world is getting younger and younger, presenting us with awesome challenges for youth and children's ministry. John Allan, an urban youthworker in the United Kingdom writes: 'The proportion of teenagers in the total population increases annually, and most of them are being born in places where the church is weakest.'[9]

ETERNAL SIGNIFICANCE

We approach youth ministry not only as sociologists and anthropologists. We come together to evaluate the challenges as followers of Jesus Christ, who reminds us that: 'Whoever welcomes one of these little children in my name welcomes me; and whoever welcomes me does not welcome me but the one who sent me' (Mark 9:37). Jesus, the voice of the voiceless, the champion of the underdog, who taught that 'the kingdom of God belongs to such as these', motivates our outreach to the young.

Our theological framework expands the way we see youth and youth ministry. At the foundation of our thinking is the conviction of the eternal significance of youth ministry. Youth ministry ministers to those in the 'hinge' years of life. The rest of their lives will swing on the decisions made during the adolescent years. Many make their personal decisions of faith at this time. In the North American context, an estimated 85 per cent of those who become Christians do so between the ages of four and fourteen.[10]

During the years we label now as 'adolescence', young people will formulate their world view, wrestle with their sense of personal purpose, determine lifestyle values, explore their sexuality, choose career direction and a marriage partner, and make choices regarding their personal faith. Life direction and eternal destiny are on the line—at a time of life when many are ill-equipped to decide. As youthworkers, we come alongside young people in these transitional years to offer the love and (we hope) wisdom that they need to make these choices.

Questions

The global and eternal significance of youth ministry presents us with a formidable task for which we often feel ill-equipped to offer answers. In the inquisitive and searching spirit of the theme, 'What is youth ministry?', I would like to build this chapter around questions rather than answers. These are questions pertaining to the global realities and multicultural challenges facing us in youth ministry in the 'big picture'. My intent is to present the challenges in the hope of setting us together in search of responses.

Is there a 'youth culture' which transcends global or other cultural distinctives? Is there a 'universal adolescent'?

In 1988, Daniel Offer and his associates produced a book based on their study of adolescents in ten different countries (Australia, Bangladesh, Germany, Hungary, Israel, Italy, Japan, Taiwan, Turkey and the United States). *The Teenage World*[11] introduced a concept they called the 'universal adolescent', a worldwide relationship of teenagers who were growing up in a similar 'culture' which has been created by a variety of forces in our world.

They postulated that music, dress and other cultural identifiers were now creating a distinct youth culture, to the point that young people in Hungary would have more in common with young people in Australia than they would with the culture of their mothers and fathers. If their conclusions are correct, the implications for cross-cultural youth ministry are staggering: rather than seeking to reach youth in individualized cultures, all we would need to do would be to identify the key entry points of the 'universal adolescent' and address our ministry to these. One standardized, globalized methodology of youth ministry could be produced for use in all the world.

Offer and his colleagues raise a fascinating possibility which any youth leader can anecdotally agree to by watching the response of teenagers in Romania to Michael Jackson, or the lines of teenagers at McDonalds in Hong Kong, Moscow, Beijing and Caracas.

But the 'universal adolescent' concept grossly oversimplifies our world. Its application may have validity for middle-class youth, but, as we'll soon see, the vast number of young people who remain untouched by traditional youth ministry in our Western urban centres or in the Two-Thirds World are economically poor. There may be aspects of youth culture affecting young people worldwide (as we'll see below), but these are usually blended into a complicated mix of traditions, local culture, family values and religious convictions.

Youth ministry in the multicultural context cannot be reduced to oversimplifications and universal methodologies. Instead, the youthworker in the multicultural context must serve as missionary, sociologist and cultural anthropologist so that the ministry is presented in ways that are culturally sensitive and relevant.

What, if any, are the common issues facing youth and the youthworker across cultures?

Although the 'universal adolescent' concept is doubtful, it is evident that youth—of all cultures and economic classes—is facing certain common challenges and influences.

Most would agree that the youth of the world is being influenced by the media. The authors of *The Teenage World* write: 'Today's teenagers share both a collective personality and a collective consciousness. They watch airplanes in the sky above them, listen to the radio, and watch a rocket launched on TV. They think of these as everyday events. A 14-year-old in Bangladesh may watch the same television programme as a 14-year-old in Germany, Israel, Turkey, or Taiwan. Media knows no borders; ideas and events are transmitted to all corners of the globe, defining what is new or desirable, and are assimilated by young minds.'[12]

They may overstate the point when they observe that 'Television may be functioning as a type of "significant other" on a global level',[13] but it is certain that the introduction of cable television and satellite dishes has intensified television's ability to spread a distorted image of life, especially a distorted image of life in the West (and more specifically the United States). Vinoth Ramachandra of Sri Lanka observes that: 'None of the American soap operas or sitcoms, for example, depict life in the decaying inner cities. The men are all wealthy, the women glamorous. Even the black families who appear are all living in the lap of luxury.'[14]

One of the side-effects of this media influence touches those in the poorest communities. In the summer of 1991, thousands of desperate Albanians (many of them young) commandeered boats to sail them to Italy. 'Apparently, one of the reasons for this exodus was that Albanians had been watching Italian television—including commercials for consumer goods, cat food being served on a silver platter and the like.'[15]

Media influence links closely with music influence, an influence that caused the writers of *Time* to conclude that: 'America is saturating the world with its myths, its fantasies, its tunes and its dreams.'[16] 'Boris Yeltsin drew 110,000 people to his historic rallies that toppled the Marxist regime; days after the coup, however, the hard rock bands Metallica and AC/DC drew 500,000 people.'[17]

Michael Keating observes the impact on one culture from the exportation of Western youth culture through music:

I spoke recently with a young man from the South Pacific island group of Fiji. He told me that life there is not the same as it was a few short years ago. Fijian youth are increasingly rebellious and disrespectful to elders, the crime rate is soaring, the drug traffic booming.

Why the change? After all, Fiji is quite remote. Television programming has only recently arrived on the islands.

His answer: American music. It arrives there as soon as it arrives here, and it has captured the youth.

What sort of life do these youth idols glorify? Animal sexuality, rebellion against all authority, violence of every kind, and party, party, party. Such a lifestyle works well for no one, least of all the rockers themselves, whose lives tend to be a mess of fear and frenzy. But the youth do not know that, and they think them glamorous and powerful instead of pitiable and despicable.[18]

Music and the media closely align themselves with what we might simply call violence-influence. Many of the world's youth are growing up in abject poverty, urban violence and in the face of war. A 1991 memo from the World Relief Commission's US office cited thirty-one countries who were living in some state of war (either internal conflicts or war with another country). In these thirty-one countries, 42 per cent of their cumulative population are under the age of fifteen.[19]

The violence glorified through the movies of Stallone, Schwarzenegger, Bruce Lee, Steven Seagal, Bruce Willis permeates into the heart of young people feeling alienated from the world and purposeless in life. The way out? Violence. Violence expresses the war raging within. Rape someone to show your superiority. Join a gang to find the family you never knew. Beat someone up to prove that you're not impotent. If you're feeling worthless, at least you can vindicate yourself by taking a few people out before you end your own life.

This violence sinks deep into the lives of young people, especially young people living in an urban-influenced world, a world that many traditional church youth ministries never touch. Luis Bush of the ad2000 Movement writes:

In the cities of the Two-Thirds world, more than 100 million children are growing up on the streets; they have no education, no affection, no adult guidance. Almost a million of them are forced into prostitution. In Bombay's 'red light' district, at least one-third of the prostitutes are little girls.[20]

Leighton Ford observes that there is no Two-Thirds World city where the median age is greater than twenty. In Mexico City, which most estimate will be the world's largest city by the year 2000, the median age is fourteen.[21] If we are serious about the multicultural challenges facing youth ministry, we must turn our attention to the urban centres. 'If the church fails in the city,' challenges missiologist Paul Hiebert, 'it will become increasingly marginal in the world.'[22]

Although the direct realities of urban life may not be touching the ministries we currently serve, the realities of youth ministry in the world will include questions such as: How do we minister to 800,000 girls under sixteen working as prostitutes in Bangkok?[23] What are the means of outreach to street kids being terminated in Rio de Janeiro by police acting like bounty hunters? Who will reach the thousands of young people growing up in the slums of São Paolo, Manila, Calcutta, Jakarta and Nairobi? These issues take us to the next question.

How, in light of limited resources, can youth ministry grow to be more holistic?

In my earliest days of youth ministry, the issues were basically sex, drugs and rock and roll, and our message was, 'Don't, don't, and do so with moderation.' Multicultural, international youth ministry is much more complicated than that. If youth ministry is dedicated to the development of the whole person—based on the holistic growth of Jesus in Luke 2:52: 'And Jesus increased in wisdom [intellectual], stature [physical], favour with God [spiritual] and favour with man [social]'—how will youth ministry respond to issues facing youth around the world?

⊙ Poverty and homelessness: 'of the 600 million people living in slums today, 74 per cent are children and young people under the age of 24' and 100 million of these are estimated to be street kids.[24]

Ajith Fernando, National Youth for Christ (YFC) Director for Sri Lanka, challenged his colleagues with a paper entitled 'Evangelizing Young People in Poor Communities'. He pointed out that: 'If YFC is to fulfill its role as a movement pioneering in reaching unreached youth, we will need to consider afresh the call to reach the poor youth of the world. Statistics may reveal that we are not doing this with much success; that, like many evangelical groups, we may be best at reaching middle-class people' (p. 3). In this paper, he highlights the fact that youth ministry in poorer communities must include relief and development work, lobbying the case of the poor before the powerful, and empowering the poor to break out of the cycle of poverty in which they are locked.[25]

⊙ Ministry among refugees, the dispossessed, the illegal immigrant: 'half of the world's 36 million refugees and displaced people are children.'[26]

⊙ Joblessness or 'underemployment': how does a holistic youth ministry respond to such needs? Literacy training? Job banks? Tutoring students so that they can graduate from high school? Providing job retraining for those stuck in 'McJobs'?

⊙ Family breakdown rendering students incapable of pursuing healthy marriage and family decisions for themselves. A vacuum of positive role models—especially in the lives of what we now call 'high risk' students—has resulted in diminished social skills.

⊙ AIDS and the epidemic of sexually transmitted diseases. What does holistic youth ministry look like in Uganda, a 'generation growing up without their parents and living in fear of AIDS'? What will the Christian gospel look like to 800,000 prostitutes in Bangkok, Thailand or a village in Myanmar where 100 per cent of the population has tested positive for the HIV virus?

⊙ Child slavery and the exploitation of youth (especially young women) as labourers, drug dealers and prostitutes. What is the role of youth ministry in defending the defenceless, offering alternatives to the desperate or empowering the powerless?

If we are serious about multicultural, global youth ministry, we will need to work and pray, and unite together to respond to these staggering realities.

How do we bridge the gap between the resources available, and the cultures and regions of our world desperately needing attention?
David Livermore, in an unpublished paper entitled 'Global Youth Ministry' cites that: 'The United States has 28 million

teenagers making up less than 3 per cent of the world's youth. 99 per cent of the paid and volunteer youthworkers in the world minister in the United States. Therefore, 99 per cent of the world's youthworkers minister to less than 3 per cent of the world's teenagers.'[27]

Whether or not the United States has 99 per cent of the world's paid and volunteer youthworkers is hard to validate, but Livermore's point—of the unequal distribution of resources—is well-taken, especially if we consider that most of the youthworkers in the United States work with middle-class students of European descent who live in suburban areas. Few dedicate themselves to the multi-ethnic 'urban war zones' where the population of youth and children is growing as a percentage of the population.

John Allan of Great Britain observes that: 'Our own failure to work in the right places, and to react flexibly in changing situations, is creating the unreached youth problem.'[28]

And how do we do this without falling prey to the temptation to translate everything that has been done in the West into other languages without any regard for culture? (How do we avoid what one author calls the 'cultural hangover' factor?)

How will youth, in any culture, be incorporated into the church?

This question raises three corollary questions: first, will existing church leaders see it as a priority to invest the church's resources in reaching out to and assimilating youth—especially when it is unlikely that these young people will actually ever become 'cost-effective', at least short-term (that is, they will never really pay for the ministry that reaches out to them)?

Second, will church leaders recognize that youth represents the *greatest challenge and the greatest resource* facing the church worldwide as we approach the year 2000? The *greatest challenge*, because young people in every culture and all over the world are living in cultures or social settings or countries where the gospel has not penetrated. We need to recommit ourselves to looking for creative and innovative ways to reach these young people with the love of Jesus Christ. The *greatest resource*, because those young people who respond to the love of Christ can be subsequently discipled and equipped to be part of the mobilized force who will complete the Great Commission of Jesus Christ. In the history of modern missionary movements, young people have always been a major catalytic factor, and a complete vision for youth ministry means seeing their potential for completing the Great Commission of the Lord, to take the news of his love to the 'ends of the earth' (Acts 1:8).

For this to occur, there must be a concerted effort of awareness building done with church leaders. A co-worker in Bogotá, Colombia identified 'consciencization' (literal translation from the Spanish) as the greatest challenge facing youthworkers with other church leaders—that is to make them aware of the needs. This presents a special challenge in those cultures where youth is not 'venerated' as it is in the West, and specifically in the United States. In many cultures, young people are expected to be seen but not heard out of respect for their elders; as a result, few church leaders in such cultures see youthwork as a priority.

Finally, will church leaders realize that getting youth from their own culture into church will be a cross-cultural experience? This is the point of Steve Flashman's book *Closing the Gap*.[29] And this is one of the points of Pete Ward's *Worship and Youth Culture: A Guide to Making Services Radical and Relevant*.[30]

These books strike at an unaddressed problem in most cultures: young people feel that they neither belong to nor are welcome in the 'adult' culture called church. Whether or not they desire to follow Christ, they still do not feel that church has any relevance to them. As a result, they often reject both the adult-culture church and Jesus himself.

There are notable exceptions. On a recent visit to six countries in South America, I noticed how youth-oriented the worship services were. When I asked the President of the Evangelical Council of Venezuela, Jacobo Miranda Garcia, what had caused the churches to respond this way, he replied, 'We do not have a youth-orientation in our worship services; most of our worshippers are youths so the services naturally take on their energy. In Venezuela (and I imagine that this is true across South America), 66 per cent of our evangelical worshippers are young people under the age of twenty-five.'[31]

Most of us, however, face two options. On the one hand, we can build youth-dominated services, emphasizing youth culture as the common denominator. In effect, we start a new denomination specifically geared to young people and the culture that they bring with them. The inbred problem, of course, is that these young people will grow older to the point that they will become the adult culture against which the next generation reacts.

On the other hand, we can try to maintain the cultural diversity and age-span representation of the body of Christ by seeking to involve youth in the church now. Rather than seeing young people as the 'future' of the church, they (and their culture) need to be incorporated in the present tense. Melchor Go, National Youth Director of the Assemblies of God in the Philippines: 'The need to channel the youth's idealism is another major concern for the church today. Young people have the imagination; they can capture a vision very quickly. Young people dare to believe when faced with insurmountable problems. David, Joseph, Daniel and Mary were monumental examples to this fact.'[32]

Summary

I'd like to close by asking one final question to which I will attempt a response: What is our mission?

For the sake of simplicity, I'd like to suggest that the greatest challenge we face in cross-cultural youth ministry is that we be *agents of hope*. Any review of the literature covering youth in almost any culture will consistently confront the word 'hopelessness'. A worker with the Mennonite Central Committee's programme on AIDS education in British Columbia started asking young people why there was so much promiscuous behavior going on even when teens were aware of the dangers of AIDS. Waldo Neufeld writes, 'I was told there is such a high level of hopelessness they really don't care; they feel there's nothing for them in the future.'[33]

In a paper entitled 'The State of Youth Ministry in Eastern Europe', David Patty examined the youth of Hungary, Poland, Romania, the former Soviet Union, the Czech Republic and Slovakia, and arrived at the conclusion that most young people are facing a hopeless future—with unemployment, unrealized dreams about freedom, violence in the streets and widespread dissatisfaction—leading to increased suicide rates and a host of other side-effects of hopelessness.[34]

In the roughest section of the city of Boston, an urban youthworker related the conversation he had had with an eighteen-year-old. The youthworker discovered that the young man was experimenting with crack cocaine. He rebuked the young man: 'Don't you realize that crack cocaine can kill you?' The young man looked at him blankly, 'Yea, so...???' A hopeless future makes a life-threatening risk much more acceptable.

In contrast to this despair comes the church of Jesus Christ. The veteran missionary to India, Lesslie Newbegin, writes: 'The distinguishing mark of this [Christian] community will be hope.'[35] He continues:

Jürgen Moltmann is surely right when he says that over the developed and affluent Western societies, there seems to hang the banner, 'No Future.' He is not referring only to the fact that millions of people in these affluent societies are not able to articulate any vision of a worthwhile future; not only to the widespread sense that we may all face annihilation in a nuclear catastrophe, not only to the mindless violence and vandalism which is a growing mark of 'developed' societies, but also to the fact that our societies appear to be intent on immediate consumption rather than on investment for the future. Just as a society which believes in the future saves in order to invest in the future, so a society without that belief spends everything now and piles up debts for future generations to settle. 'Spend now and someone else will pay later.'[36]

Through relationships, love of students and a willingness to imitate Christ by coming into the world of those we're trying to reach, we come as agents of hope. God's hope. Hope of forgiveness. Hope that I can change, that you can change, that our world can change by the power of the gospel.

Ajith Fernando of Youth for Christ, addressed this in his summary of the 'Youth Track' at the Lausanne II Conference in Manila in 1989:

Many participants in Lausanne II came to realize that
young people need human leaders like Jesus who can be
role models for them. They need someone to teach them
how to show unselfish, loving, and creative concern for
those less fortunate than themselves. Young people need
loving, kind, and gentle leaders who can understand
their deepest longings, and yet guide them into a
radical community stripped of race and class barriers.
A bewildered and fractured generation is searching for
meaning in life.[37]

Vincent Donovan, a missionary to the Masai people of East Africa, wrote a profound book published in 1978 entitled *Christianity Rediscovered*. In his reflections on the purpose of missionary work across cultures, he observed: 'there is no future tense in the Masai language... I think you could say that one of the purposes and goals of evangelizing the Masai is to put a future tense in their language.'[38]

And this is our challenge across cultures and countries in reaching youth: *to give them a future tense*, a hope, a sense of future, a sense that life has meaning and purpose and is worth living. In the face of violence and unemployment and challenges and fear, the voice of God rings forth through those dedicated to love young people and exemplify the optimism of faith: 'For I know the plans I have for you. Plans for welfare and not for calamity, to give you a future and a hope' (Jeremiah 29:11).

NOTES

1. Gordon Aeschliman, 'The Internationalization of the Gospel', *ESA Advocate*, April 1991, p. 14.

2. Speaking at a Missions Conference in March, 1993, both Dr Bill Taylor of the World Evangelical Fellowship Missions Commission and Dr Tite Tienou of the Christian and Missionary Alliance Seminary in Abijan, Côte d'Ivoire noted that this dramatic and historical shift had taken place.

3. Bryant Myers, The Lausanne Letter, November 1994.

4. Mark Senter, 'An Historic Perspective of Children/Youth Ministries and World Evangelization' presented September 23, 1992 at the EFMA Mission Executive Retreat, p. 13.

5. By 'traditional' youth ministry, I am referring to youth ministry that has arisen in response to the Industrial Revolution, after which societies began to recognize the creation of the 'adolescent' phase as we know it, a period where a young person is neither child nor adult, or, better, is

physiologically an adult but sociologically undefined. This theme is studied in Ronald Koteskey's *Understanding Adolescence* (Victor Books, 1987). Mark Senter of Trinity Evangelical Divinity School, in the paper cited above, 'An Historic Perspective of Children', identifies several cycles of children and youth ministry beginning in the early 1800s. He sees the post-World War 2 increase in youth-oriented ministry as the 'Youth for Christ Cycle' (1941–87). He sees us entering a new cycle, a cycle no longer focused on the 15 per cent of the youthful population described as student leaders or aspiring student leaders: 'The new paradigm of ministry to children and youth will scrap the model orientation and will place its creative energies on developing and empowering adults to identify, establish contact with, and minister to a wide variety of sub-populations within the under fifteen population.'

6. Stephen Hoke, 'Introducing World Vision International', *Evangelism*, Winter 1988, p. 73.

7. Bryant Myers, 'The State of the World's Children', *The Great Commission Handbook*, 1995, p. 80.

8. Statistics vary, but *Britannica World Data* (1987) as well as the 'PC Globe' software list Botswana, Kenya, Jordan, Zimbabwe, Mayotte and the Marshall Islands as having populations which are 50 per cent under the age of fifteen.

9. John Allan, 'New Strategies For Reaching Unreached Youth', *Evangelical Missions Quarterly*, April 1988, p. 131.

10. This data comes from Lionel Hunt's *Handbook on Christian Mission* and is confirmed by research done by Frank Mann of Child Evangelism Fellowship and evangelist Harry Trover. Source: W. Benke and M. Bryan, 'The World's Most Fruitful Field', *Evangelizing Today's Child*, 1977.

11. Daniel Offer, *et al*, *The Teenage World*, New York: Plenum Press, 1988.

12. Offer, *The Teenage World*, p. 115.

13. Offer, *The Teenage World*, p. 116.

14. Vinoth Ramachandra, 'The Honor of Listening: Indispensable for Mission', *Evangelical Missions Quarterly*, October 1994, p. 405.

15. Matthew Connelly and Paul Kennedy, 'Must It Be the Rest Against the West?', *Atlantic Monthly*, December 1994, p. 62.

16. The Leisure Empire', *Time*, December 24, 1990, p. 56.

17. Terry Mattingly, 'Ten Questions that Depict Your Kids' Culture', *Youthworker Journal*, Winter 1994, p. 98.

18. Michael Keating, 'The Stolen Generation', *Pastoral Renewal*, May, 1987, p. 15.

19. Based on a World Relief memo dated 19 March 1991 and the population statistics of *Britannica World Data*.

20. Luis Bush, *Funding Third World Missions*, Wheaton: The World Evangelical Fellowship Missions Commission, 1991, pp. 12–13.

21. Leighton Ford, quoted in Ted Engstrom's *Seizing the Torch*, Glendale, CA: Gospel Light/Regal, 1989, p. 206.

22. Paul Hiebert, 'World Trends and Their Implications for Missions', *Trinity World Forum*, Fall 1990, p. 2.

23. Myers, 'The State of the World's Children', p. 81.

24. Myers, 'The State of the World's Children', p. 80.

25. Ajith Fernando, 'Evangelizing Young People in Poor Communities', presented at the Youth for Christ International Convocation in Chicago in July 1993.

26. Myers, 'The State of the World's Children', p. 80.

27. David Livermore, Calvary Baptist church, Grand Rapids, MI: 'Global Youth Ministry'.

28. John Allan, 'New Strategies', p. 130.

29. Steve Flashman, *Closing the Gap*, Eastbourne: Kingsway Publications, 1988.

30. Pete Ward, *Worship and Youth Culture: A Guide to Making Services Radical and Relevant*, London: Marshall Pickering, 1993.

31. Personal visit on 16 November 1994.

32. Quoted in Kate Tampol, 'How Are Churches and Youth Ministries Equipping the Youth of the Land?', *Evangelicals Today and Asia Ministry Digest*, July, 1994, p. 12.

33. Quoted in Bramwell Ryan, 'Forever the Same, Yet Changing', *Faith Today*, July/August 1994, p. 20.

34. David Patty, Malachi Ministries, 'The State of Youth Ministry in Eastern Europe', 18 May 1992.

35. Lesslie Newbegin, *The Gospel in a Pluralistic Society*, Grand Rapids, MI, Eerdmans, 1989, p. 101.

36. Newbegin, *The Gospel*, p. 112.

37. Ajith Fernando, 'Youth: More Than Half of the World', *World Evangelization*, Summer 1989, p. 31.

38. Vincent J. Donovan, *Christianity Rediscovered*, Maryknoll, New York: Orbis Books, 1990, p. 78.

6

The body language of Christian youth ministry

SIMON HALL

This chapter is about body language—about the secret messages that people give off to one another without using words. Although we're often wrong, we instinctively follow our first impressions when we meet someone for the first time: their dress, stance and facial expression, even their accent, all help us build up a picture of that person without us ever listening to a word they're saying. If we are in the communication business, we are trained to give over a positive image using such things as posture and tone of voice to ensure that what we say is heard. Nonetheless, sometimes our body language reveals things about us that we'd rather not let anyone see, or that we weren't really aware of ourselves.

I work for three local churches, helping them to plan and organize their youth ministry. Much of what we do is fairly standard: youth groups and clubs, small discipleship groups, uniformed organizations, residentials and so on. I'm really quite proud of what goes on. I think we were quite good at evaluating and developing what we do. Yet one day, a chance conversation with the editor of this book made me ask myself a fundamental question: What does all this stuff tell young people about God? If you like, what is the body language of my youthwork? This question is, I think, important for all of us to answer for two reasons: firstly, there is much we can do to improve God's image simply by means of human thought and effort. Just as public speakers can learn to change the way they speak (Mrs Thatcher is a famous example), so can a church-based youth ministry change its style. There are plenty of books on this so I am not going to cover it here at all, and anyway I am personally more interested in the second reason, which is this: some of the deep-seated beliefs that inform our youth ministry (our body language) can sometimes only be discovered by observation of what goes on.

A simple example: we have a regular meeting called 'AZ', which aims to attract non-church young people who are willing to discuss social issues and find out what Christians think about them. When we have any upfront teaching, I try to have group discussion and feedback or say that people are free to chip in or ask questions and, for a time, this worked quite well. Recently, kids have been more reluctant to join in and I ended up asking some of them why they were so reticent. They told me (I really wasn't fully aware of this) that when people say things, I nearly always make a little joke about them, so most people didn't want to get up and talk because they were afraid of being made to look a fool. Oops! My words said that I valued participation but my 'body language' was contradicting that completely.

A writer named Robert St Clair has said that we have two theologies (some people aren't sure they have one!): a 'classical theology', which is what we have been taught and say we believe, and an 'operational theology', which is our actual body language as Christians.[1] St Clair, who died in 1990, used to run workshops in which he would force people to come to terms with the differences between their stated beliefs, and what their actions and attitudes said about their *real* beliefs. Often in this simple process the Holy Spirit was working, bringing repentance and a new hope. This chapter, while obviously based on my own personal experience, is intended to bring about reflection that will allow our youth ministries to undergo a similar conversion experience.

Because space is limited, I am going to explore one particular theme as a case study of how we might reflect on our practice as youthworkers. In the middle of 1994, three of the most senior leaders in our church returned from the Airport Vineyard in Toronto, where they had received prayer ministry and been affected by God in a way that could not be mistaken. As in many other churches in the United Kingdom, there were significant after-effects of this. While rejoicing in what God was doing through this movement, I soon began to feel that somehow God was limited by our own expectation of what he could do in the world and this caused me to ask myself the same question: What does the youth ministry based at this church tell young people about God's interest and involvement in their lives and worlds?

The churches I work for are very much part of the charismatic stream of UK Christianity. We sing songs that proclaim both God's love for us as individuals and his power to change the circumstances of our existence. We preach from the Bible that God has given us a mission and a destiny to fulfil which requires radical personal renewal. There can be no doubt that one of the key emphases that the charismatic movement has restored to the church is the notion of God's presence with his people and action in the world. Along with most evangelicals, charismatics would say that God is active in the world, yet I find that this 'classical' theology is not reflected in the 'operational' theology of the churches for which I work.

I think the best way to explain it would be to think briefly about our own attitudes to two famous verses from the Bible: 'The earth is Yahweh's and everything in it' (Psalm 24:1) and 'Satan is the prince of this world' (John 12:31). From our reading of the Bible, we must assume that, in some paradoxical way, both of these statements are true, but when we watch the news at night or see a child playing in the street, what are we thinking? Do we see the world as a place of God's presence and activity, where the Holy Spirit is constantly preparing the way for us; or is the world an evil place, requiring of us that we set ourselves apart, feeding on the Spirit at church in order to survive the rest of the week? I suspect our body language communicates the latter, no matter what is in our hearts. Below is a description of a national charismatic church:

[This movement]... is noted precisely for the manner in which it has been able to secularize and make authentic its worship and piety. This is a community that is concerned with the body (God wants to cure not only the

soul, but also the body; sin has not only alienated humanity from God, but also robbed it of its physical health). This community is neither ashamed of nor offended by the musical instruments, songs, and dances of its cultural setting, but rather incorporates them into its worship and consecrates them to God. This is a missionary community, yet it suffers from a profound religious and missional alienation. God can save individuals, but not society. The world can be brought to the church, but the church cannot be in the world. The church, therefore, cannot and ought not to become incarnate in its social situation. It must always be at the service of mission (always preaching), but never at the expense of the church building.[2]

This is a description of the charismatic church in Chile, around the time that thirty-two of its most prominent leaders signed a declaration of support for the oppressive Pinochet regime. The author, Costas, argued that although the theory *and* practice of work that the church was undertaking was undoubtedly biblical, it was undergirded by a wonky view of the world which meant that the Chilean Christians were unable to be '... as innocent as doves and as wise as serpents' (Matthew 10:16) in that particular situation. Because their view of God's kingdom was so other-worldly, they were happy to get into bed with a dictator simply because he would favour them over the left-wing Catholic Church.

Perhaps we feel that the church in this country would never be so naive, but I still remember many Christians saying that we should vote for Mrs Thatcher's government because of fears about how Labour might restrict religious freedoms in this country. I suspect that a church which devalues the world tends to damage more than just itself.

But how did we get to this point? In this century, the evangelical movement in the United Kingdom was in decline until the 1970s. Christians in this country got used to having decreasing social impact and either retreated into Christian ghettos or developed the so-called 'social gospel'. Within Christian youthwork, this happened as well,[3] although this has never been perceived as a significant issue because youth ministry grew up in a time when Christianity was already under siege.

I believe that our body language as Christian youth ministers suggests a profound imbalance in our attitude to the world, partially caused by this history. So much of church youthwork looks like an attempt to save people, not from sin, but from the horrible world 'out there'. And indeed, that is what many are paid to do. My own contract of employment is presently being reviewed. After initial discussions with the relevant people in the church, a proposal was brought back to me which included the suggestion that I spend 80 per cent of my time on 'church-based work'. This wasn't even work with church kids, but time spent on projects *in the building*. Needless to say, after a cup of tea and a long chat things were sorted out and a common understanding established. However, this is an issue where we are in danger of inflicting damage on more than just our image, because an operational theology which sees God only in church will automatically see only evil in the world. As Christian youthworkers we meet kids on the street or in school and we represent an organization which says: 'the world you live in is bad, leave everything—your friends, your music, your fashion—and come to church.' Surely we shouldn't be surprised that Christians are generally described by such words as boring, out of touch and judgmental.

At this point I need to add a little balance to my argument. When I was at school, those of us who were Christians tried really hard to witness according to John 13:35: 'By this shall all men know that you are my disciples: that you love one another.' Unfortunately, we ended up loving one another so much that we hardly knew anyone else in the school. My point is that we were, I hope, godly in our intentions but unwise in our actions. I feel this about the charismatic movement: that we are so enthusiastic about what God is doing with us that we are unable to stop and think about what *we* are doing. The verse just mentioned is a clear indication that Jesus was aware of the importance of what I'm calling body language: some things are not only done for their own intrinsic value, but also for the impact that they have on others.

So, if the analysis is right, how can we put the situation right? How can we learn to express a belief in an active God who cares, in both word and deed? As I have searched for a form of spirituality and theology that matches my experience of meeting God in the world of young people, I have been encouraged by the writing of a number of contextual theologians.[4] In marked contrast to books written by charismatics,[5] I found in these writings people who started from the presupposition that God is *out there*, calling us to do mission *where he is already*. There was a faith in God's ability to do works in the world that I found lacking elsewhere. Yet this faith was in God's ability to work with the material provided, namely us, rather than having to zap us from his far-away throne. The motif and metaphor used were incarnation. Not only did God become flesh in Jesus, but he is incarnated in the world today. In my own thinking, this one particular image has helped me to see how I can understand (and explain) God's activity in the lives of young people. It has also brought about a few changes in the way that things happen in our youth ministry. In the two and a half years since we began to work through some of these issues, we have seen significant growth in numbers of people contacted each week (from around forty to around 300); but I should say that numbers of committed Christians haven't grown nearly so much (from around twenty-five to forty-five). Below are some of the thoughts and ideas that we have been playing with in an attempt to improve our own body language as we try to get some of the young people we know 'into Jesus'.

The image of the incarnation can have great power both for the youthworker and the young person. If matter can truly be the dwelling place of God, the world of the young person too can be a place where we find him. Rather than seeing young people as simply 'lost' and needing instruction, we can choose to see God working in and through them. Put another way, when we disciple young people, are we making something or growing something? If making, then it is right that we manipulate the materials provided to achieve the desired outcome. If growing, our job is that of waterer, as we wonder at the power of creation. There can be no doubt that at times we want to make our young people into Christians, and that's hardly surprising. When a young person comes to me with a question, I fear being unable to answer. Somehow I've got the idea that it is my job to make that young person's faith for them.

We recently took thirty church kids away for a weekend to study the book of Micah (they chose it!), yet we had no talks. All the work was done by the young people, reading, discussing, checking out something in a commentary... when our time was over, it was clear that God had come close to them in their struggle to own their faith. For those who came who weren't from a church background, the rough and tumble of discussion and debate, and finally coming to a decision about something came more naturally. For all of them, what they had learned was theirs: Jesus the truth (John 14:6) was incarnated in their lives.

If we are talking an incarnational kind of language, the idea of following Jesus becomes a little less unreal. We have been trying out the idea of an annual work party for both Christians and non-Christians (thanks to Phil Wall for the original inspiration). These, and the more traditional mission weeks that kids take part in, we explain are part of 'doing the business with Jesus'. When we pray for young people we try to avoid imagery that speaks of a distant God firing bolts of blessing from out of the sky. Instead, in our prayers and songs we are attempting to evoke pictures of God and us together. When the Holy Spirit comes, he hasn't just got off the 2:10 from Kings Cross. He was here all the time, but we just didn't know it.

Most of our church young people live in a twilight zone between the church and the world, so we have asked new converts and non-Christian kids to tell us how we should be doing our youthwork. By giving those on the fringes the opportunity to influence our work, we can hear God say things we might never have heard otherwise. Simple things like allowing 'raw' young people to lead meetings can make a real difference. Venues and meeting times can be important. I recently heard of a youth group that met early on a Saturday night in the town centre, so everyone could go out on the town together afterwards.

We also need to remember what we already know about how people come to faith. Those who are not from a church background (and many of those who are) nearly always say that friendship was the main reason they became a Christian. We should never lose sight of this simple fact. If the presence of Christians in the world can have no other purpose, let this be it: to show the love of Jesus as real. We need to allow ourselves to be present in the world of teenagers as a sign of Jesus' presence. The way I personally do this is to visit young people at school. Over time, I have built up the trust of the staff at the school so that I am able to walk round the school, visit the sixth form centre, and so on. For the Christian kids in the school, it is a reminder to them that God is there, for those who aren't Christians, I am a sign that somebody might care. One of the results of my presence has been a renewal of activity among the Christians in the school. The flagging Christian Union was shut down and a group called 'The Underground' formed, praying before school for the needs of its members and more generally for the school. They are planning events that will 'give Jesus a good name' in the school, such as Traidcraft stalls, a mission, and so on This is really encouraging!

I know that there are many churches all over the country doing all this and more. I'm not advocating a policy of trendy activism. What I am trying to suggest is that we tell ourselves the truth about what we're doing and ask others to do that for us as well. Perhaps we should try to find out what the young people we know think we are trying to communicate and what we inadvertently communicate. They know better than us the kind of gospel we're really preaching.

We are living in a time when young people are looking for some new ways of living. If we can get our body language right, I believe that many will find following Jesus to be the only way of living.

Appendix

Here is a questionnaire to help you examine your group body language.[6] Get together with the youth team in your church and work on the following questions. You may like to use a simplified version with young people. What is your group like? In answering the questions below, try to think of specific examples of what you are saying.

⊙ How do people describe the group *metaphorically*? What pictures do you and others have of the group?

⊙ What is the physical impression of the group? Where does it meet? Are there special artefacts that are used (for example, an overhead projector)?

⊙ What are the official and unofficial values of the group (for example, official: 'everyone is equal in this group'; unofficial: 'the leaders are more equal than others')?

⊙ What are the important dos and don'ts? What is really praised and what really condemned?

⊙ Are there any important rituals in your group (that is, 'we always...').

⊙ Is there a special language that people have to learn? This may be religious or not.

⊙ What are the stories people tell? What are the most important memories?

⊙ How are people rewarded or punished? What for?

⊙ What is the favourite topic of informal conversation (for example, once the meeting is over)?

⊙ Who are the important people in the group (present or not)? How do they symbolize what the group is about?

⊙ How does the group break down into subgroups or cliques? Are they in harmony or conflict? Does one have more approval than another? How do they affect the working of the whole group?

NOTES

1. R. St Clair, *Co-discovery: The Theory and Practice of Experiential Theology*, Bibal, Berkeley, 1991, p. 171.

2. O. Costas, *Christ Outside the Gate: Mission Beyond Christendom*, Orbis, Maryknoll, 1982, p. 50.

3. See Pete's Ward's 'Distance and closeness: finding the right ecclesial context for youthwork', chapter 3 above.

4. See particularly, C. Kraft, *Christianity in Culture: A Study in Dynamic Biblical Theologising in Cross-Cultural Perspective*, Orbis, Maryknoll, 1980.

5. See particularly, M. Green, *I Believe in the Holy Spirit*, Hodder & Stoughton, London, 1975, pp. 58–75.

6. Adapted from G. Morgan, *Creative Organisational Theory*, Sage, London, 1989, pp. 297–298.

7

From parachurch to metachurch

DAVID HOWELL

Introduction

In our work with young people we regularly encounter a basic truth—that young people do have time to talk about things spiritual, even about Jesus and God, but they have no time for the church. They see it as irrelevant, boring and full of hypocrites.

We all know this. The book *Reaching and Keeping Teenagers* quantifies it and we organize our evangelistic activity from that perspective.[1] We keep 'the church' well in the background, we focus on people, on God, on Jesus and begin to struggle when they have come far enough in their commitment to the faith to need to be integrated into the church.

Such is the reality of the work that we do with young people. But the danger is that in identifying with the young people with whom we work, we can subconsciously take on board their approach to church. In doing this we can run the risk of an unbiblical understanding of the church which can then colour our own thinking when we consider how to take young people on through the fourth dimension of evangelism, discipling them into the faith and into the faith-community—which is the church.[2]

This development has given rise to much activity in the area of culturally relevant youth worship, youth congregations and youth churches, but before we can engage in that area, we need to understand what should be the biblical relationship between youthwork and the church, especially when that youthwork spans a number of local churches.

Throughout the history of the established church there have been structures which have sought to focus the work of the kingdom in particular ways or in particular areas. These are the organizations which have lately been called parachurch organizations.[3] The questions which face us today are: Were there parachurch organizations in scripture? Is there a biblical mandate for their existence?

It is the contention of this chapter that to describe the relationship of an organization, such as Youth for Christ (YFC), to the local church as *parachurch* is not biblically valid or accurate. It is more appropriate, and biblically more correct, to refer to YFC as a *metachurch organization*—a part of the church, accountable to the church, serving the church and networking together those committed to youth evangelism.[4]

The current situation

This century has seen a prolific rise in the number of parachurch organizations. In the *1993/4 United Kingdom Christian Handbook* there are over 4,000 organizations listed in this country alone.[5] Most of the organizations have come into being through a particular perceived need because either the church was seen as failing to meet the need, or it was felt that another structure would be more appropriate.

From this a tension has arisen between local churches and parachurch organizations. From the parachurch perspective the church has been seen as being unable to move fast enough, or creatively enough to meet the needs of a changing world. From the local church perspective the term parachurch has sometimes been used in a derogatory way to describe an inferior work which will one day return to the fold. There are some places where local churches have recognized that a parachurch structure has been the best way to engage in ecumenical activity, bringing Christians together for specialist work. In other places local churches have viewed the parachurch as a law unto itself staffed by individuals who will do their own thing regardless of what the church may say. Some parachurch organizations have seen the church as reactionary, staid and a thing of the past.

Because of this, it is important to build up a biblical model which will enable both local church and parachurch to understand how God intends his work to go forward in his way. In the past twenty years, there have been two important approaches to the issue of how the two should relate. One has been the development of the 'para-local church' model and the other has been the development of the 'modalities-sodalities' model. But before we can examine these models we need to be clear about the nature of the church to which we are seeking to relate them. We have already seen that it is easy for culturally relevant youthworkers to 'rubbish' the church; however, we need to recapture the biblical high ground upon which the church should stand.

The church—a divine/eternal organism

Whilst struggling with the present reality of church life, it is important that we should still hold the concept of and outworking of church in the highest regard. The Bible has a high view of the church. You have only to read Ephesians to see the way in which Paul viewed the church. It is 'the body of Christ'—the living presence of Jesus here on the earth (Ephesians 1:23). When we come together to be a church, we are not just a bunch of folk, we actually become the very living body of Jesus. We are baptized into Christ/the church, we have Jesus living in us and we come together to be Jesus living in the world.

The one who established the church is Jesus Christ himself. In Matthew 16:18 Jesus said 'on this rock foundation I will build my church, and not even death will ever be able to overcome it.' The church belongs to Jesus, he is building the church and the church will not be destroyed by death, whether his or ours.

This means that it is part of the eternal structure of the things that God has created. It will not pass away when heaven and earth pass away. Let us be careful not to knock the church; for all its weaknesses and inadequacies, God has an eternal plan for it and I would venture to suggest that it will survive for a lot longer than current youth culture.

We are God's very household; we are to be those in whom the eternal truth is made real in our society. 'This letter will let you know how we should conduct ourselves in God's household, which is the church of the living God, the pillar and support of the truth' (2 Timothy 3:15).

This desire to regain a high biblical view of the church is hampered and made difficult because so many churches do not have a correct view of what they are and what they exist for. However, our task here is not to decide how the church should behave itself, our task is to live in a correct biblical relationship with the church. Living within the church according to the word of God will, I believe, have a profound effect (Isaiah 55:11).

In Romans 12:10 we are urged to show proper respect to one another in the church. In 1 Thessalonians 5:12 we are to pay proper respect to those who work amongst us. And in 1 Peter 2:17 we are to respect everyone and love our fellow believers

Having sought to understand more clearly how God sees the church, we now need to examine how organizations engaged in the mission of the church should relate to church structure.

From parachurch...

The problem with analysing the para-local church model is that there is, to my knowledge, no theological work currently published in this country which seeks to explain the concept. I have, therefore, had to work second-hand to present what I hope will be an accurate summary of the phrase.[6] The term parachurch usually refers to an organization which stands 'alongside of, by, near or parallel to' the church. It can refer to any specialist body which seeks to fulfil a particular activity on behalf of the church, but which is not seeking to be a church in its own right.

In order to understand this and the other models in this chapter, I have used a visual representation of parachurch taken from Jerry White's book, *The Church and the Parachurch*.[7] The model is presented in graphical form on page 94. Local churches are represented by the circles which contain Bs and Us. This implies that they contain both believers and those who are not yet believers (unbelievers), which is what we would expect.

The large circle represents the universal church which, according to Jerry White, the author of the model, equates to the body of Christ. Because God alone knows who is in the universal church and who is not, he alone knows where the line goes through each church. In addition, it is argued that there are believers who exist within the body of Christ, but outside of a local church. This is justified by 'the lonely pioneering missionary who does not have a local church to fellowship with', 'the man who received the gospel on his death bed', and the dying thief on the cross. All are seen as part of the universal church but, for varying reasons, they are or were not in membership of a local church.[8] From this it has been argued that just as individual believers can exist on their own outside of local church life, so too groups of believers can exist outside, and alongside, the local church.

In this model local churches are seen to have a very general task: 'the local church's calling necessitates a certain

The Relationship of Local Churches
to the Body of Christ

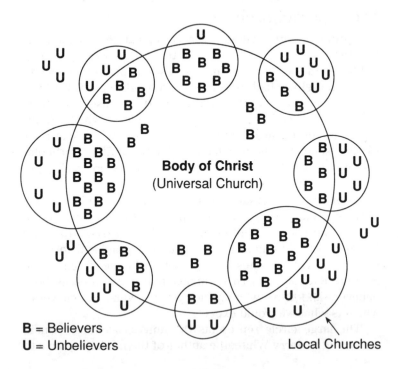

B = Believers
U = Unbelievers

generalism. She must reflect every aspect of christian responsibility. She must have a comprehensive agenda including worship and the sacraments, teaching and christian nurture, evangelism, pastoral care and social concern.'[9] Specialist structures are needed to fulfil a calling to reach particular people groups. Therefore, parachurch organizations can carry out specialist work that local churches cannot. In the model, parachurch and local church are seen on a par. 'Both YFC and the local church are legitimate expressions of the church universal.'[10] Thus a more accurate description of the model is of a para-local church organization.

But the model is flawed in that it allows too great a space to the exceptions. It is a fact that there are those who come to faith outside the local church, but it is to the local church that they are then directed and within which they need to be discipled. Ajith Fernando in the YFCI Position Paper states clearly that: 'Our mission is to disciple him [an unchurched young person] into the local church.'[11] We all know that those who come to faith need to come into a valid expression of the faith-community which is the church.

The model gives the impression that it is possible to have an existence outside the local church, floating free like a neutralized ion. But the lonely pioneering missionary is 'sent out' by a local church and supported by that fellowship. The dying thief on the cross did not have time to visit all the local churches and find the one that suited his new-found theology. He entered the kingdom within minutes or hours of his conversion.

The New Testament does not concern itself with legalizing structures in regard to the local congregations. The prime 'structure' in which it is concerned to see conversion and spiritual growth is that of relationships. Each person who enters into a relationship with God automatically enters into relationship with others who are in that same relationship to God. It is a relationship which is to be lived daily and totally. There is no sense of being a 'free agent'. Wherever the people of God come together, there they are the church—the local being a microcosm of the universal.

The model also has a flawed argument in justifying a generality from a peculiarity. Whilst it is recognized that there are a few circumstances where individuals will not necessarily be part of a local church, it is not justified to move from the existence of individuals floating free to the concept of a group/parachurch being a free grouping of people not connected to a local church. It seems to me that this is the weakest point in the argument. You cannot equate single saints with multiple conglomerates!

In addition, to restrict Paul's phrase 'the Body of Christ' just to a universal understanding is not possible. It is clear that in his first letter to the Corinthians Paul addressed the term specifically to the congregation in Corinth which was receiving his letter (1 Corinthians 12:27): 'All of you are Christ's body and each one is a part of it.' In order for it to refer to the universal church he would have had to extend the context and say 'You and all the others across the world are Christ's body.' Paul does not appear to separate the church universal from the church local in that way. He sees just the church, whether it is expressed locally or globally.

With regard to authority and accountability this model does allow parachurch organizations to be autonomous structures—making them semi-accountable to the universal church. However this effectively means that they are independent organizations, as there is no organized leadership of the universal church to which they can be held accountable. Whilst Paul was clearly independent, he chose to live in relationship with the other church leaders of his day and was prepared to submit to them when necessary (Acts 15).

... through modalities and sodalities...

Ralph Winter has, in various publications, sought to develop an alternative model which seeks to define the two structures of God's redemptive mission—modalities and sodalities (affectionally nicknamed 'mods and sods' by Youth for Christ staffworkers at their conference in January 1994). His argument was that for the church to grow, it must have these two structures and they must 'work together harmoniously for the fulfilment of the Great Commission, and for the fulfilment of all that God desires for our time'.[12] In order to discuss his approach I have sought to translate his argument into a model using the same basic structure as Jerry White for parachurch.

Modalities are 'a structured fellowship in which there is no distinction of sex or age'.[13] In this he includes structures such as the Jewish synagogue and the New Testament church. These are modalities which anyone can enter into and which provide the basic units of fellowship and relationships within the faith. The church through the ages has had modalities—primarily the local church and the denominational groupings. Ralph Winter regards these as the static dimension, the bottom-line of commitment. The implication of his argument seems to be that if they had existed on their own they would not have been able to revitalize themselves or extend the kingdom, and would have slid towards oblivion if they had not been stimulated by the sodalities.

Sodalities are 'a structured fellowship in which membership involves an adult second decision beyond modality membership, and is limited by... age or sex or marital status'.[14] In this, Winter sees the dynamic dimension of God's redemptive mission. Paul's missionary team was a sodality, separate from the local church, moving freely to establish new churches. Ralph Winter argues that in later centuries the monastic movements became the driving force (sodality) of church life during the medieval period. Certainly many orders were evangelistic and were active in evangelism prior to, and following, the Reformation. In 1792 William Carey established the first modern Protestant sodality when the Baptist Missionary Society came into being.

The sodalities, then, are the specialist agencies, the coming together of enthusiasts whom God uses to achieve his work here on earth. The modalities are the all-embracing structures. Ralph Winter argues that each needs the other, for together they are used by God to build his kingdom.

In the diagram on page 98 modalities are seen as local churches (the circles) or as diocesan or denominational groupings of churches (dotted lines joining groups of circles together). Sodalities (triangles) would be parachurch or denominational structures seeking to stimulate and motivate the church or churches as indicated by the arrows.

Ralph Winter argues that we need to be: 'clear that God, through His Holy Spirit, has clearly and consistently used another structure other than (and sometimes instead of) the

A Model of the Relationship Between Modalities and Sodalities

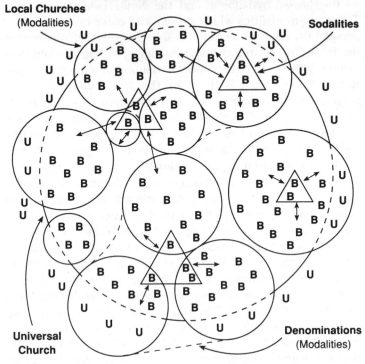

Local Churches (Modalities)

Sodalities

Universal Church

Denominations (Modalities)

modality structure. It is our attempt here to help church leaders and others to understand the legitimacy of both structures, and the necessity for both structures not only to exist but to work together harmoniously for the fulfilment of the Great Commission, and for the fulfilment of all that God desires for our time.' [15]

The model is valuable in that it seeks to liberate our thinking from the narrow confines of believing that God can only work, and will only work, through the existing church (modality) structures. It also gives us a model within which to better understand Paul's missionary activity (sodality) and the work of missionaries and evangelists through the ages. Any study of church history reveals that God is active in history and does not restrict himself to working only with one structure, the local church (modality).

In analysing the misunderstanding of sodalities that has arisen in contemporary Christianity, Ralph Winter appears to argue that the great missionary endeavours of the nineteenth century 'degenerated' (my term) in time from sodalities to modalities as they allowed themselves to be influenced, controlled and then dominated by ecclesiastical structures. In noting the way the denominational missionary societies began, and then, as they waned, the 'faith missions' began, he draws our attention to a number of basic truths which are generally accepted by those who analyse organizations.

One such truth is that people like to be in control. Church leaders like to be in control of their flock and in control of any other semi- or parachurch groups who might be working their 'territory'. In the same way, sodality leaders have realized the control they can have over their own work outside local or national church government. This has made the formation of parachurch organizations an attractive option to those who have been frustrated by the slowness and reserved nature of the decision-making processes within the modalities. It has also meant that a tension can develop between the leadership of the sodalities and the leadership of the modalities. The basic issue is one of accountability. Is the sodality accountable only to itself or to others?

For any sodality to remain fresh and vibrant within God's economy, the group has to be open continually to God's creativity and 'new thing'. Within a sodality there must be a dynamic quality—the 'dunamis' Spirit—which keeps the group ever wanting to move forward. In Youth for Christ, as one of the wave of youth sodalities which broke into existence in the 1940s, we must be constantly aware of avoiding rigid structures and always ready to respond to the work that the Spirit is doing. We also need to be aware of when our work may be finished, and when we might need to dissolve this sodality and make space for a new one to come forward.

Ralph Winter argues that it is possible for a sodality to cease to be effective by having 'cooled down' to a modality. This implies that there is not a simple polarity of structures, but a spectrum. He begins to recognize this when he writes: 'it is important to note, however, that the average Mennonite or Salvation Army community, where whole families are members, typified by the desire for a "pure" church, or what is often called a "believers'" church... constitutes a most significant experiment in Christian structure. Such a structure stands, in a certain sense, midway between a modality and a sodality, since it has the constituency of the modality (involving full families) and yet, in its earlier years, may have had the vitality and selectivity of a sodality.'[16]

While sodalities and modalities might express the extreme positions, there are more points in between than Ralph Winter allows. A better way to phrase it is to see the two positions not as basic structures but as the two ends of a spectrum of God's redemptive mission.

The New Testament does not allow us to define clear categories of activity in the way that Ralph Winter suggests. The work of God was breaking out in many places, and the style of Paul's church planting was different from that of Peter as he worked with the churches in Asia (1 Peter). What does link them is a form of first-century 'apostolic-networking' activity. The apostles in Jerusalem were busy co-ordinating and linking together the various new fellowships and new activities of the kingdom as they sprang up around them. The gospel was being proclaimed by evangelists, lived by those in the faith-communities and the apostles were linking it all together. Relationships were being established, the vine was being 'dressed' and they were voluntarily submitting to one another (Ephesians 5:21).

Both the models we have looked at so far are challenging to our thinking, but I believe that both fail adequately to pick up the biblical pattern in the New Testament church. Our task now is to move...

... to metachurch organizations

The New Testament is the story of the Good News incarnated in Jesus. It tells how that Good News was spread to almost every part of the then known world. The church grew and expanded through the activity of the Holy Spirit. It sought to fulfil the mandate that Jesus had given, which was to go and make disciples. In general the New Testament uses the term 'church' both in the sense of particular local congregations (as per Acts, James, 3 John and Revelation)—an assembly of God's people belonging to a certain geographical area; and in the sense of a universal church—the church of God across time and space. The structure was still fairly fluid as the church grew at a phenomenal rate and sought to come to terms with the necessary organizational systems.

In addition, the New Testament used a large number of cognate expressions for the church, for example the 'people of God', the 'messianic community', the 'Body of Christ', the 'fellowship of the Spirit' and many others. The writers sought to express the coming together of those who were in Christ. The church was seen to be physical and corporate, finding true expression when people were together in Christ. The important point was that it was not possible to provide a single definition of the burgeoning organism that was the 'church' but it was recognized that *every believer belonged to the church*.

When the persecution of the church began and the witnesses were dispersed from Jerusalem there was still a real sense that the new work was accountable to Jerusalem and the apostles. When Philip went off on his evangelistic tour, some of the apostles in Jerusalem followed on to sort out and clarify the problems (Acts 8:14f.). He appears to be in fellowship with the sending church—the central Jerusalem church, and his work is submitted to them. (See also Acts 11:19–24 for a similar example.)

When Paul set off on his missionary journeys, he appeared to retain a relationship with the sending church but did not appear to be under the same constraints as Philip. He was sent off as a result of prayer and fasting by the elders of his church in Antioch (Acts 13:1) to whom he reported back at the end of the mission (Acts 14:27). When Paul wrote to the church in Galatia fifteen years later he was at pains to point out that he was not under orders from the Jerusalem church in his missionary activity (Galatians 1:15–18). However, when the fundamental issue of cimcurmcision arose in Antioch (Acts 15:1) Paul and the others referred the matter back to the apostles in Jerusalem. They were prepared to submit themselves and be accountable. The important point is that it was not required of them, but they gave themselves to this relationship.

From these and other incidents we can argue that Paul's view of the church was that of each person living in relationship with other Christians in a local area and a networking of believers universally. (I am convinced that Paul would have had much greater problems with our plethora of local churches in one geographical area than he would with the existence of para-local church organizations.)

In the various missionary activities recorded in the New Testament, there was a coming together of people from different local churches into a grouping for evangelistic and missionary activity. Paul and Barnabas were sent out from Antioch, Timothy from Corinth, Luke joined them at some point (as per the 'we' passages in Acts), possibly in Troas. As Paul's missionary activities continued we could include other specialist missionaries from other local churches who were coming together in this task. This, then, is the biblical mandate for an inter-church activity which has a specialist nature—in Paul's case that of evangelism and church planting. This inter-church activity is characterized by a networking of specialists, and by their maintaining relationships both with their sending churches and within the local churches where they worked. Hence the use of the term metachurch—a part of the church, from within the church, accountable to the church, serving the church and networking together those committed, in our case to youth evangelism.

The diagram on page 103 seeks to illustrate graphically the model of the relationships between organizations and the church that existed in the New Testament, and should exist today.

Jesus Christ is the centre of the church, both locally and universally. He is the head of the church and Lord of all. The outer circle represents the universal church and the segments of the circle represent local churches. Every B represents a believer; the church then consists of believers who are in relationship with one another locally and who are automatically part of the church universal. Every U represents an unbeliever and the aim is for them to move into fellowship, into Christ. The segments extend beyond the line of the universal church because (a) only God knows who is in the universal church by his grace and (b) the church exists to draw all into faith.

The church is an open community which exists to incarnate Jesus and enable all to hear the Good News. Whilst it is not represented in the diagram (for the sake of clarity), it is understood that there is a dynamic movement from the outside, through commitment, towards the centre and becoming like Christ. In fact the diagram could be seen as a cross-section of a spherical model where there is a dynamic movement towards the centre. Each believer is not seen as static, but as growing into the likeness of Christ (Ephesians 4:15–16). In the diagram this would mean moving to the centre of the circle.

A metachurch organization, such as Youth for Christ, is represented by the believers (Bs) in various churches who link up with one another, as represented by the dotted line. The metachurch organization is a networking of those in fellowship with local churches coming together within the universal church to do a specialist work; in our case, seeking to draw

A Model for the Relationship Between Youth for Christ and the Church

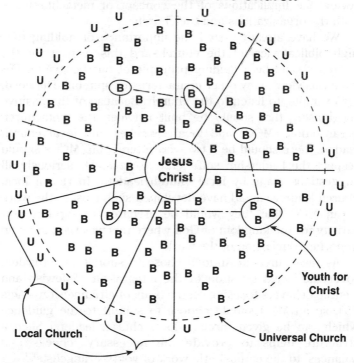

young people into a relationship with God and discipling them into the local church from within the local church.

I believe that Youth for Christ should no longer refer to itself as a para-/outside the local church organization, but a metachurch organization which works alongside and from within the church, bringing together those who have been called into youth evangelism. It emphasizes the 'coming from' aspect of Youth for Christ as it comes from the churches to reach young people and see them grow into faith within a local church. I believe this model more accurately reflects the biblical pattern of the networking of specialists in relationship to and with all the local and national churches.

The implications for the metachurch organization

In the same way that the writers of New Testament letters bound practice into theology, so it is important quickly to review the implications of the concept of metachurch for both the organizations and the church.

We have already stated the importance of holding to a high biblical view of the church and this respect for the church should be a guiding principle of our behaviour. For from this view many other characteristics spin off. The need, for example, to listen to the church. Because of the positive relationship that should be built between the metachurch organization (MCO) and local churches and local church leaders there should be a two-way interaction. MCOs should respect the leadership sufficiently to consider seriously all suggestions made by local church leaders. In return local church leaders should have developed such trust in the work of an MCO that they would be prepared to support new activity for the kingdom of God where this was seen to be an important dimension of the work.

As the church in Antioch chose to submit to Jerusalem (over the vexed question of the integration of Jewish and Gentile believers focusing on the issue of circumcision—Acts 15), so an MCO should choose to submit to the guidance which can be given through local church leaders. Such a structure helps to provide the necessary 'checks and balances' to the enthusiastic work of youth evangelists! [17]

Within Youth for Christ we believe that every worker, whether full-time, part-time or volunteer, should belong to a local church. In addition, that church should regard the worker's calling as a calling from within that fellowship. This means that the worker should be cared for pastorally and spiritually, and that each should be accountable as individuals to the leadership of that church, even as Paul and Barnabas reported back to their sending church and other churches (Acts 14 and 15). And when a new worker is placed in an area, it would be important for that worker to build relationships with a local church in the same way that Paul did when he travelled round preaching the gospel. Pastoral care works best in a local setting.

We are clearly called in scripture to serve the church. Jesus established the way we should live when he said 'the Son of Man did not come to be served; he came to serve and to give his life to redeem many people' (Mark 10:45). The pattern established by Jesus and picked up countless times through scripture is one of positive service. This is not servitude, a demanding activity to make us feel like slaves. Biblical slave/servanthood is a strong concept, requiring us to do our best because we do it for God and not for man (Colossians 3:23). I choose to be a slave/servant to Christ and through him to his church, he does not force me (as when Mary makes such a commitment to God in Luke 1:38). It is not for the church to require us to be servants, it is for us to make this commitment to the church.

By the very nature of their missionary activity, Paul and Barnabas challenged the understanding of church that had arisen in the minds of many Jewish-Christian believers (Acts 15:1). Like it or not, part of our role in relationship to the church is to bring a challenge—to allow what God appears to be doing among unchurched people to have an impact on the church, lifting us out of our complacency and forcing us to ask the question: Is this what God is doing today? Such a role is not to be desired, nor is it easy, but it does appear to be biblical!

The result of the foregoing is a willingness on the part of metachurch organizations to be accountable to the church. The history of their origins as parachurch organizations is that the church has not been doing the job, so a group have pulled out from the church to get on with the work. To pull out beyond accountability does not appear to be biblical. To retain a relationship which allows interaction of thought and prayer appears, both pragmatically and spiritually, to be far more healthy. The problem for national organizations is how that accountability can be realized nationally. I simply hope that this chapter will stimulate the outworking of a scriptural policy.

The implications for the church

In the same way that there are implications for the MCO, there are also implications for the church, the first of which is to *release* people into MCOs. When the church believes someone is called to serve through an MCO, then it must trust them to go out and present the Good News. The church needs to express a willingness to release them for this work. This is exactly what happened when the church in Antioch met in prayer and fasting, as recorded at the beginning of Acts 13, and this is a pattern that should be picked up in every church. Our society has become far too individualistic for its own good, and our churches reflect this tendency. Too few people are in this work today because their church came to them first and said, 'God has told us that you are to go out in his name.' What happens is that you and I have to go to the church to ask it to check out what we believe God had said to us.

A further hinderance to the mission of the church is its 'siege' mentality. Almost every church I know is jealous of its members and will not allow anyone out to do anything else. We have created such complicated internal structures that the church appears to be a sociological black hole—sucking people into events, committees and responsibilities. The church is called to send people out into service for the kingdom. The visual image should not be that of a black hole, rather it should be a springboard.

Whilst there were some believers who did not trust what was happening with the growth of the early church—as witness those from Judea who turned up in Antioch, and started teaching that Gentiles had to be circumcised and effectively become Jews before they could become Christians—there is in the New Testament a great sense of trust in the evangelists who went out. God's Holy Spirit was moving so powerfully that people were prepared to go with it. The doctrine of the church grew from the work of God, rather than the work being hindered by the structure as is the case today.

Throughout the New Testament there was a terrific sense of support for the work of outreach. Fasting, praying, laying on of hands, sending off into the work (Acts 13:1f.), and then catching up with all that happened on the return (Acts 14:28). For Paul and Barnabas, their local church was the group which loved and supported them through this time. So much so that when the apostles went to Jerusalem to sort out the problems concerning the circumcision of Gentiles 'it was decided that Paul and Barnabas and some of the others in Antioch should go to Jerusalem and see the apostles and elders about this matter' (Acts 15:2). They were not left to fight their corner on their own. And then when the company returned from Jerusalem, it was not with an appropriate piece of paper, but with the support, backing and physical presence of 'two men who were highly respected by the believers' (Acts 15:22). (Oh, that the church today would support us to this extent, that it would be prepared to fight our corner for the sake of young people who need to know the Good News of the kingdom!)

Their support also indicated their ownership of the work. This was not something that Paul and Barnabas went off and did in isolation from the church. No, there was a specific commitment to and identification with them and their mission (Acts 13:3). The work of the metachurch is the work of the church. This needs to be the church's approach today, to own the work, and to be committed to the work and the workers.

As a result of what God was doing through the work of Barnabas and Paul, the church reviewed its policy and made changes. It decided not to force all Gentiles to become Jews first, but to encourage habits that would be mutually acceptable. Oh, that the church of God would listen to what we are saying about young people and change what it does in the light of our experience! Then there would be no need for us to talk about setting up youth congregations or youth churches. The church itself would be choosing to change and would become the 'keeping church' it is meant to be.[18]

Conclusion

As a result of all that has been said, it is clear to me that there is no biblical justification for parachurch organizations where 'para' is seen as being separate from the local church. I believe scripture calls us to the concept of metachurch organizations, a part of the church, accountable to the church, serving from within the church and networking together those committed to youth evangelism.

It is hoped that such an approach to the interconnectedness of Youth for Christ with the churches will remove suspicion, build relationships and result in an expansion of the kingdom as more and more young people come to know Christ. In this way it will enable Youth for Christ to fulfil its mission which is 'to take Good News relevantly to every young person in Britain'.

NOTES

1. Peter Brierley, *Reaching and Keeping Teenagers*, Monarch, 1993. This book brought together research into young people's attitudes to the church; especially the reasons why an average of 300 young people left the church in England each week during the period 1979–89.

2. 4-D Evangelism is part of the strategy of Youth for Christ to engage in a holistic, biblical evangelism. It sees the four main areas of work to be demonstration—showing the love of God through works and wonders; declaration—enabling young people to hear the gospel message clearly; decision—moments which allow a young person to make a commitment; and discipling—the continuing process of enabling a new believer to become 'like Christ'. A position paper is available on this topic from YFC.

3. The term parachurch is not a technical theological term. It is a phrase which has come into Christian jargon in the last twenty years. The definition of *para* according to the Oxford English Dictionary (2nd edition, volume 11, Clarendon Press, Oxford, 1989) is 'by the side of, beside, alongside of, by...'. The first recorded use was in the *Guardian Weekly* (12 December 1970): 'groups that don't attract or seek publicity, that meet in upper rooms... this is sometimes called the parachurch, the church of the future which is beginning to take shape.' *The Church Times* (17 December 1976) states: 'The author shows that the 'underground' churches that sprang up in the late 1960s have rightly given place to a new form—namely the 'parachurch' or alternative church—which exists alongside the institutional church.' From its beginning as meaning what we now call the 'house' or 'new' churches, the meaning has changed to refer to any Christian organization which is not a church! As far as I can see there is no definition of the term in the theological dictionaries published in this country.

4. The genitive use of the New Testament Greek word *meta* can mean 'with them, from within' and is a much more accurate description of the relationship that should exist between organizations such as YFC and the church. I decided on the term *metachurch organization* before being

aware of the phrase 'metachurch' which has been used by Carl George of the Fuller Institute. In his book, *Preparing Your Church for the Future* (Fleming Revell, 1991), he takes the Latin meaning of the term 'meta' 'to change' and applies it to the culture of a church. The church has to change its way of thinking and working in order to make it easier for people to enter into the life of the church and into faith. He describes this kind of mission-based church as a metachurch. Eddie Gibbs refers to the concept in his book, *Winning Them Back* (Monarch, 1993). In correspondence over the possible confusion for people between the two uses of the term Eddie Gibbs sees a value in its use in referring more accurately to parachurch organizations. In discussing what metachurch means he goes on to refer to our concept and say, 'it seems to me to strengthen your argument. I have never been happy with the term *parachurch* as I believe that "church" in the New Testament embraces both the local Christian community and the apostolic band (or mission agency).

The definition of *meta* in the Oxford English Dictionary is 'sharing, action in common; pursuit or quest; and especially, change (L)'.

It seems to me that a metachurch is one where missiology is defining ecclesiology. The idea of a metachurch reaching out in relevant ways into the community in order to enable people to be drawn into the life of the church seems to me to be the basis of a metachurch organization—where we are seeking to do together in the community that which can best be done together for the sake of the kingdom of God.

5. The *United Kingdom Christian Handbook*, published by Christian Research Association every two years.

6. The description of parachurch and the visual representation used come primarily from a Youth for Christ International position paper written by Ajith Fernando—position paper 3, 'Our Context' (YFCI: Singapore, 1985).

7. Jerry White, *The Church and the Parachurch*, Multnomah Press, Portland, Oregon 1983 and used in Fernando's position paper to which all references are made.

8. Fernando, 'Our Context', p. 3.

9. Fernando, 'Our Context', p. 2.

10. Fernando, 'Our Context', p. 3.

11. Fernando, 'Our Context', p. 4.

12. Ralph Winter, 'The Two Structures of God's Redemptive Mission', in *Missiology: An International Review*, 1974, pp. 121–139. Reprinted by Pasadena: William Carey Library.

13. Winter, 'The Two Structures', p. 124.

14. Winter, 'The Two Structures', p. 136.

15. Winter, 'The Two Structures', p. 130.

16. Winter, 'The Two Structures', p. 130.

17. This is the basis for the 'council of reference' which every local YFC ministry establishes, enabling the local church to oversee the work.

18. The term 'keeping church' comes from YFC's strategy. It is the belief that it is possible for a church to become a place where young people can enter, can believe and grow in the faith and stay through the difficult adolescent years. For more information see the position paper 'Keeping Churches', available from Youth for Christ, Pioneer Centre, Cleobury Mortimer, Nr Kidderminster, Worcs. DY14 8JG.

Further reading

Ajith Fernando, 'Our Context', Youth for Christ International Position Paper 3, YFCI: Singapore, 1985.

David Howell, *YFC's Relationship to the Church*, Youth for Christ.

Jerry White, *The Church and the Parachurch*, Multnomah Press, Portland, 1983.

Ralph Winter, 'The Two Structures of God's Redemptive Mission', in *Missiology: An International Review*, 1974, pp. 121–139.

Ralph Winter and Pierce Beaver, *The Warp and The Woof*, Pasadena, CA, The William Carey Library, 1970.

8

Models of youth ministry

COLIN BENNETT AND DAVE ASTILL

When one looks at church-based youth ministry today, there is a wide variety of methods or models used. There are many and various books and other resources available to youthworkers in church-based ministry, offering both ideas and ways of carrying out their ministry. So why should the question of the biblical nature of those so-called models be raised and that nature evaluated? We, as the church, are desperately seeking new ways of working to meet the changing demands of discipleship and outreach in today's world, particularly the world of youth subcultures. Pragmatic models of 'doing youthwork' may be fine in the short term, but will they last? Are they biblically focused, theologically sound, and will they remain therefore when held up to scrutiny?

Stereotypes of church-based youth ministry

How do we make sense of the variety of types of youth ministry and the programmes we see exhibited in the church today? Duffy Robbins has said, 'There is no shortage of proposals about how youth programmes should be designed. The youth ministry landscape is littered with programmes that were built and cannot be used. That is why it is worth looking critically at the various models of church youthwork programmes.'[1] To look at youth ministry programming is one thing, but what we may need is a radical appraisal of the biblical basis of youth ministry types, and what they are producing. To assist in analysing the current trends in church-based youthwork, it is possible to review a few of the models more prevalent in the United Kingdom by means of stereotyping. We can then ask whether there are some key ideas we can trace, and whether these stereotypes can be called biblical.

If you asked most people what church-based youth ministry was about, they would answer from one of two general cultural modes: the first is what can be called 'traditional church culture', and the second can be called 'radical alternative culture'. In using these terms, we must be careful to know to what we refer.

TRADITIONAL CHURCH CULTURE

This is not confined to any particular denomination, or historical length of church-based ministry. It is the perspective which underlies many of the churches in which youth ministry exists, and where many of today's youthworkers have tested their calling and developed their skills. Outlined below are seven stereotypes of those pragmatic positions adopted in this view of church-based youth ministry:

'Look after them for us'—babysitting

With the young people out of the way, the adults have the freedom to worship God in their church services. The actual intent may not be to relegate the youthwork to this function, but the attitude of the church as a whole may be structured to meeting the spiritual needs of the adult congregation, while the young people's programme consists of little more than very basic teaching and, indeed, time filling. There is often little practical difference between the children's teaching and that provided for young people, except in the fact that for the older groups, the material has been 'aged' to suit the recipients. Little regard is held for the value of adolescent spirituality.

'Look after them instead of us'—surrogate parenting

In this scenario, the job of parenting and nurturing young people through adolescence is transferred to the youthworker. Often the youthwork team will be expected to perform everything from teaching and discipling, through to total emotional support and discipline. The parents may not ever be interested in knowing what the young people are saying, nor in detail what their children are receiving—until something goes wrong! The youthwork programme is expected to provide all that is required to present the young people as mature adults at the end of their time within the church youthwork.

'Make them like us'—generational cloning

The young people are taught to become 'Christians like the adults', in keeping with the church traditions. This is by no means confined to the more historical denominations. As a response to the changes (some may say threats) of popular youth subcultures, the church as a whole would like to continue as it has done in producing mature adult believers. Part of the process is perceived to be the 'production' of young people in the same cultural setting as the adult congregation. The youthwork resembles a microcosm of the whole church life in culture and personality.

'It's party time!'—enjoy being with us

The focus is on the enjoyment and popularity of 'being here', 'in' and not 'out'. For some churches, the perception of the necessity of large numbers and a good image works itself out in youthwork which inadvertently plays upon the natural drive to 'belong'. There can be a compromise of what would be a radical biblical message, in order to attract to the church group by competing with what is already on offer. There can be a deliberate move towards promoting the exclusivity of membership.

'Working from *my* agenda'—this is my group

This type and the one which follows spring from the question of who is setting the agenda, and who 'owns' the group. Here, the youth ministry team owns the group, sets the programme, and the young people work within those set confines. The development of Christian discipleship stems from the perceptions the youth leadership holds of the young people within the church. Although some notice is taken of the desires of the young people, the direction, aims and content are set by the adult leaders. It is fair to say that this model will resemble closely a traditional schooling method.

'It's *your* group'—the youth ministry facilitator

By contrast, the reverse happens in this type of ministry. The ideas will come from the young people, the youth team facilitates the programme and then stays in the background as the young people carry on. Responsibility for the direction of the work often remains with the leadership, but they will not necessarily have a major function in controlling the content of the programme. It can be said to be the youthworker equivalent of 'surrogate parenting'.

'Forget the church kids, let's save the real young people'—the mission mind-set

Although this forms part of a church-based youth ministry, it is in all respects totally focused on those young people who know nothing about Christianity, and leaves the church kids to church. Many of the stereotypes will include outreach to unchurched young people, but this form will tend almost to ignore any member of a church family or churched young people. There is a constant move towards evangelism, with discipleship occurring within the church family, as a consequence of the youthwork outlook.

RADICAL ALTERNATIVE CULTURE

This is the second cultural perspective. It can be found mainly in churches which have made some analysis of contemporary youth culture, and are seeking to meet the needs perceived. Again, we could stereotype seven models. We have been helped by Duffy Robbins' work, as he seeks to categorize work by Mark Senter and Doug Fields.[2]

'The hero'—natural teenage appeal

'As a bright light night attracts students, so will those students attract other students... and so on, like so many moths buzzing around a street light.'[3] The focus is often around a key personality, be it the youth minister or worker or, more rarely, a young person. A friendship with this person is a status symbol within the ministry, and discipleship is found by working with this person. It is a response to the rise of the cult of personality, seeking to provide a suitable role model as an alternative to those already on offer in society. The young people may seek to establish themselves as mirrors of the style of leadership, with a view to acting as attractive people to friends and others.

'Involvement'—joining the team

Almost as a parallel to 'It's party time!' in the first section, this ministry is built from event-oriented teams of young people. The ministry is developed around specific activities or functions, for example dance, juggling, drama, music, evangelism or community action. The work among young people is carried out within these smaller task-oriented groups. Developing youthwork among the larger ministry as a whole falls more to those who plan the strategy of how these groups may function together and complement each others' productions.

'If it's new, it's good'—the must-be-relevant group

This type of ministry can often result from an awareness of needs expressed by young people, and where there is a desire to deal with those issues as they arise. Rather than there being a preset overall strategy for the youth ministry, the focus is on the felt need. The group and work exists to meet the issues of the day, concentrating wholly on practical lifestyle matters. The Bible may not be the focus for authority or relevancy: indeed, where the focus is on the here and now, the Bible can often be declared 'old', and therefore 'irrelevant'.

'Bambi versus Godzilla'—Spring Break versus King James

'Spring Breaks' are high profile events drawing big crowds, strong on excitement, but weak on content. So rather than there being a regular series of meetings, or a planned programme for work with smaller groups of young people, the trend is towards larger-scale high-energy events, really providing high points of activity. At the other end of the scale, so-called 'King James' methods emphasize 'heavy-duty discipleship' and Bible study, without any of the perceived frivolity associated with events. There is a tendency towards strict doctrinal orthodoxy and seriousness in such a ministry, and perhaps also a rejection of those unable to cope with what can be received as an academic approach.

'Boot camp'—get your hands dirty!

Falling somewhere within the elements of 'Involvement' and 'Bambi versus Godzilla', this emphasis is upon young people becoming actively involved in Christian service—work projects, missions and service to the world. The youthwork is directed to training for the practical outworking of all the teaching and information which is available to the young people. The test of discipleship can be the amount of effort exerted or the number of projects adopted by the individual young person.

'The only radical alternative'—the youth church

This can be a popular alternative, whether or not there are adult congregations in an area. To build up an indigenous church where the young people are, with a style of worship comfortable with the subculture of young people in the area, can be a successful way of keeping young people within the influence of the gospel.

'The biblical warrior'—the New Testament church lives!

Some churches have taken a mandate from the Acts of the Apostles, and have brought the focus of their youth ministry into that domain. Young people are called forward to be filled with the Holy Spirit and empowered by God to demonstrate their gifts in evangelism, through friendship, street campaigns and higher-profile ministry within the wider congregation. A direct comparison is made between their work and that of the early church, testing and validating the ministry of the young people by the demonstration of the spiritual gifts revealed in the New Testament.

So here we have fourteen models or methods, drawn from the traditional church and the radical alternative cultures, shaping what is seen today within church-based youth ministry. What about their biblical nature?

A biblical framework

If we are looking at biblical material, what are the key imperatives which we must consider? The gospel presents us with a number of given facts: God's holiness and love, humanity's sinfulness and separation, and God's offer of restoration in Christ. How we seek to communicate this today is a matter of pragmatism. 'Pragmatism' has often been more of an accusation within Christian circles, but how did Jesus approach people? In a variety of ways, according to their situation and condition, to bring the Father's love to them. This was, and is, inconsistent in the eyes of the world and church, but true to the nature of the Son of God. What we are challenged by is a consideration of, and return to, *biblical pragmatism*.[1]

When asked by John's disciples (Luke 7:18–23) whether he was indeed the Messiah, Jesus did not go into an explanation of his methods or credentials, unlike his discourses with the Pharisees. He asked them to look at what he was doing and its effect—was the kingdom of God reaching humanity? Linking this with his teaching in Matthew 7:20, 'Thus, by their fruit you will recognize them', we are given a practical demonstration of how to approach and go about our ministry. Paul saw and practised this, becoming, for the sake of Christ, 'all things to all men so that by all possible means I might save some' (1 Corinthians 9:22).

Another biblical concept key to our thinking is that of *incarnation*. Doug Stevens[5] has expounded this clearly, that just as Jesus was involved with people, so we should be involved with young people. We should be prepared to talk about and demonstrate the secret of the gospel, with its healing, restoration and encouragement. Our ministry must also demand the right to be heard, but earn that right by the giving of our lives in faithful service. The cost to us is the laying down of our lives. The gospel we are giving is not merely of words, but of life, which should be both the motive and the aim of our ministry.

As Terry Dunnell puts it in his publication *Mission and Young People at Risk*, our ministry is carrying out God's intentions among forsaken young people. Clearly then, models for church-based youth ministry must be missiological, incarnational and culturally responsive; by that we mean they must be transforming culture, rather than being against, or subsumed under, culture. The whole issue of the interplay between youth ministry and youth subculture is one we must all consider, but is outside the scope of this chapter. Yet in essence, as youthworkers, we must be people who are redeeming the culture in which we live.[6]

This incarnational imperative, then, encourages us to explore other familiar passages which we propose simply to highlight here. Reverting to the earlier reference to Luke 7, Jesus was himself making reference to his address in the synagogue in Luke 4, the Messianic mission of bringing liberation to the poor and oppressed. In this context, the validation of the ministry of Jesus was the effect the kingdom of God was having through his ministry. It was much wider than a performance-related approval, and deeper than the end justifying the means. Quite the reverse: Jesus proclaimed that the kingdom of God could be brought into the world, and then went on to demonstrate it. His aims and objectives were stated and performed.

Jesus also emphasized the necessity in the ministry of his disciples of prayer, power and practical help in Luke 11. This was confirmed by the prayer offered to his Father for his followers, recorded in John 17. Christ prays that we shall be united in love and obedience—an inspiration for us in our ministry, and also in our awareness, that we should be open to God to listen to his answer and should respond in obedience to his call. Coupled with the challenge brought by Matthew 25, this encourages us to discover compassionate service among those who suffer. This passage in itself shows the variety of ways the gospel can be brought to the world.

In Ephesians 4, Paul brings to us the importance of the ministry of all believers, where each has a unique contribution to make, without being envious or possessive about what God has given to each in his will. Some see this passage as setting out the biblical model which should be reflected in youth ministry, where the team has each of the specific persona there mentioned—apostle, prophet, evangelist, pastor and teacher. However, isn't this passage more of a job description than a model for ministry? All these functions are essential within the body of Christ for it to be complete in carrying out the commission. This speaks both to the church ministry/youth ministry relationship, and the youthworker/young people relationship. One cannot divorce the youthwork in a church fellowship from the wider ministry of that fellowship.

Our mission imperative is found in familiar passages in Matthew 28 and Mark 16: making disciples of all people; proclaiming the good news; driving out demons; and healing the sick. Where the church was carrying this out, the lifestyles of the believers reflected the coming of the kingdom into everyday life. The lives of the believers are shown to us in Acts 1–2, which look at witness in the power of the Holy Spirit; Acts 2:42–47 talk about living together with all things in common. The characteristics of lifestyle and ministry working together present to us a challenge as to our own living of ministry.

Where we return to is the discussion between Jesus and John's disciples. The ultimate test and validation of our ministry is whether we are carrying out the messianic mission imperative in our youth ministry.

Critique

Let us return to the thought in the first comment from Duffy Robbins. Is the search for the perfect model of church-based youth ministry actually a valid, biblical search? Are we asking the right question? Is 'model' the correct word in the search? From what we have seen of the ministry of Jesus and the early church, we should begin to have doubts. Grantley Watkins, of Aylesham Tabernacle Community Church, warns us of the dangers inherent in the search for methods, be they from 'traditional' or 'radical alternative' cultures. 'The Holy Spirit makes structures work; he is the glue that cements. Structures will only work if they are in line with the Holy Spirit... With methods it is easy to become self-sufficient.'[7] He draws our attention to Moses and Joshua crossing the Red Sea (Exodus 14), and Joshua crossing the Jordan (Joshua 3). A similar problem was presented in both situations, but the same method was not used—even though Joshua was involved on both occasions. What were used were faith, relationship and revelation.

Are we prepared to consider the risk of no longer seeking to rely upon methods of youth ministry in themselves? Recently in Auckland Cathedral, New Zealand young people were invited to design and produce a new tapestry for an area inside the building. The result? A biodegradable tapestry, which will last approximately ten years, and then will need to be replaced. A design for the times, but which does not unhelpfully tie the future with the past.

Where we may have fallen down in the past is in confusing 'model' with method. Looking at the fourteen stereotypes of youth ministry, what we have looked at are *methods* of ministry. Do not take away the impression that the authors are anarchistic in their approach to church-based youth ministry, or are thoroughly jaded with current methods! Far from it. We are both involved in youthwork teams, in quite different church settings. Youth ministry cannot progress unless we have thought carefully about our strategy: How are we to fulfil the biblical mandate for youth ministry if there is no means of putting it into effect? Without a structure, those ministries would not function. The concern of this chapter is to look at youth ministry in the church context, and examine even the underlying foundations of what we are about. Where we are heading in our thinking is to a realization that there is a vast difference between *reliance upon* methods to communicate the gospel effectively to young people, and the *use of* those methods.

In each of those stereotypes, there are good points and bad, some more obvious than others, and no two fully suited to the same situation. It is highly unlikely that any church would fit wholly and exclusively any one of them. Yet what they challenge us to do is see the strengths and weaknesses inherent in the theory and practice of each, and learn from them. We should make ourselves aware that a method is only useful when it is aiding the aim of the ministry by facilitating, clarifying and providing secure boundaries, to name but a few benefits. Yet if we do not have an aim for our ministry, then the method or its structure can dominate. If a subtitle were to be given to this chapter, it would be something like: 'Looking at what I am doing, is the aim of my youth ministry biblical?' For unless we have defined our aim within our ministry, we shall be aimless! The biblical material allows us to consider whether our current aim is in line with the word of God. Once we have worked on this, then we can begin to look at our method.

A word of caution here about working to define our aim: there can be a temptation to seek to do everything within our youth ministry, or indeed an expectation that this is what we will do. That is why the strategy for youth ministry must be an integral part of the overall strategy of the church family.[8] To have a clear aim under the guidance of God's Spirit, and then to be diligent in carrying it out, will be not only more rewarding in many ways, but it will also be easier to see whether it is being achieved. And if it isn't, then evaluation can take place. We should not be frightened of evaluating our ministry against a biblical aim, as without this what would we be doing? Even in the biblical passages explored here, and the emphasis we have placed upon Luke 4, we must realize that this is just one of the many aims we can find within scripture. For some churches, the aim may seem narrow, for others, broad. Yet if we are obedient to God in the community we are serving then that difference is ultimately insignificant. We should also be prepared for the unexpected gifts of God in changing our aims. We should not fall into a success-oriented syndrome. We are aware that Christ's strength is made perfect in our weakness: so, to an extent, we should be looking to our 'weaknesses' before God, rather than to our strengths. So the elements of being flexible before God, being obedient to his command and taking biblical risks in our ministry should be encompassed within our understanding of a model of ministry.

So what of methods? We must have an aim, and we must have a strategy for putting it into action. One can find some justification for the maxim, 'A precedent is a good servant, but a bad master.' Returning to the theme of biblical pragmatism, too often the temptation is to see success elsewhere, and transplant the method into our own setting, making a few adjustments as necessary for our abilities. What our reflections show is that this is the wrong way round. Learning from the experience and ideas of our fellow youthworkers is essential, but just as Jesus treated each situation and person individually, so we should be challenged to be creative in the practice of our ministry. We can draw on other methods, but then review our context, the young people, and our calling from God before dashing into action.

Is there such a thing as a 'model' of youth ministry? There is: the ministry of Jesus gives us the perfect model of relational ministry, which is really where we should be looking. As we are dealing with the lives of people, our effectiveness will depend upon our relationships with them and with each other. Jesus dwelt heavily upon the importance of who people are in the kingdom of God, and his many methods all focused on the importance of the person. We go back to who we are before God, the calling he has made upon us, and the value that God has placed on the young people among whom we are called to minister the love of Christ.

Concluding questions

In seeking to evaluate our ministry biblically, we must ask ourselves several questions about our approach within this framework: methods, motives and mission.

⊙ What assumptions do we have about young people, ministry direction and our calling? Have we tested them against scripture?

⊙ What is the aim of our youth ministry? Are we in fact containing, controlling, maintaining or cloning?

⊙ Is the messianic mission of Luke 4 present in our youth ministry?

⊙ What is the relationship between our church community and the unchurched community? Is there evidence of links and interaction in our youth ministry?

NOTES

1. Duffy Robbins, 'More than a Meeting', *Youthwork Journal*, Summer 1992, Youth Specialties.

2. Robbins, 'More than a Meeting'.

3. Robbins, 'More than a Meeting'.

4. John Chapman, 'Moving into Mission', Seminar, Wimborne, December 1994.

5. Doug Stevens, *Called to Care*, Youth Specialties, 1985.

6. H. Richard Niebuhr, *Christ and Culture*, New York: Harper and Row, 1975.

7. Grantley Watkins, New Frontiers International Conference, November 1994.

8. Peter Idris Taylor, 'Towards a Theology of Youth Ministry', *Baptist Youth Ministry Youth Specialist Journal*, 1992.

9

The year of Jubilee: a pattern for youth ministry

ANDY HICKFORD

The North Atlantic in winter is desperately, desperately cold. At night not only are your extremities numb, but your bones ache. As I stood on the deck braced against the wind, I replayed in my mind the events of the last half hour. Our tanker had been about its usual business trudging through rough seas when the bridge received a mayday call. It was far from clear, but from what we could make out there was a fire on board a trawler, fishermen were abandoning ship and it was a desperate cry to anyone in the area for assistance. Fortunately, we heard their position and knew we were close. Such was the thought of men in the water on a night like this that any orders were hardly necessary. In fact, the ship had started its slow process of altering course long before the command was given to turn.

We put the searchlights on and despite the cold all the crew came up on deck. Some tried to pierce the all-enclosing darkness with powerful lanterns, others strained to hear something above the noise of the wind and sea, but most gave vent to their feelings of utter powerlessness and quietly cursed the speed of the ship.

After what seemed like hours (but was in reality only a few minutes), we suddenly picked out, in the shadowy area of the spotlight's arc, the distinctive orange of an emergency life-raft. There were shouts from the men around me, part relief, part fear at what we might find and, as we drew closer, numb hands started to make our rescue boat ready.

Slowly, we began to make out figures clad in yellow oilskins and orange life-jackets, huddled together in their raft. Hands were raised and waving, but not as normal men would; it seemed like slow motion, more like the exaggerated actions of drunks. Their desperate exhaustion was obvious to us all.

I found myself bundled into our rescue boat and as the winch began to lower us down I heard the orders given over the tanker's Tannoy to cut engines and drop the anchor.

As soon as we hit the water I felt it. The current was incredibly strong, the tide was literally racing by. In a matter of seconds we reached the life-raft and instinct took over. We knew these men were all in; some groaned, some murmured, others didn't move. Exposure was so advanced that life or death was now down to a matter of minutes. We worked like crazed men. Grabbing hold of the line, we hauled against the current and finally got the boat alongside—and then it was bedlam. It was a question of getting hold of something, a life-jacket, an arm, a leg, even someone's hair and pulling, dragging, scrambling with all your might until they were on board. At last we had everyone off and wrapped in blankets, but they needed urgent medical attention back at the ship's sick bay to stand any realistic chance of survival.

I turned and, as I did, became aware that the light we had been working in had almost faded. What I saw filled me with horror. The current was so savage it had already carried us at least a quarter of a mile from the ship. With the size of the lifeboat's engine and the number of people on board, it would take us ages to get back. I knew instantly that these men would never survive the journey. Gripped with fear, I shouted for the ship to move towards us, but it was hopeless... they just couldn't hear.

For the past eight years I have been in the lifeboat of Christian youthwork and, however supportive the mother ship of the church has been, ultimately it is locked onto a different course. The journey from culturally relevant youthwork to the traditional voyage of the church, against the tide of culture, has time and time again proved to be too far for many of the young people we have worked with.

This chapter is a call to the mother ship of the church to hold unswervingly to its destination, but to alter the course it takes in getting there. In addressing the subject of 'The year of Jubilee: a pattern for youth ministry', I first want to make two introductory comments about the title:

⊙ **It lacks a question mark!** Some comments in this chapter must be seen as descriptive and not prescriptive, (as yet anyway!) My aim in writing is not to give you a colour by numbers package, but rather to grab your imagination and leave you with questions about the relevance of Leviticus 25 for institutional Christianity today.

⊙ **Youth ministry: the prophetic edge of the church.** This chapter is written on the basis that, if youthworkers discover a way forward for their work with young people, its principles can be applied beneficially to the wider church. As Michael Eastman has written, 'The experiences of Christian youthworkers have a prophetic word for us all.'[1]

Let me explain what I mean. The problems of the Western church are enormously complex and, even at the local level, notoriously difficult to grasp. Fraught with denominationalism, relational politics, individual church history, community expectations and individuals' backgrounds, the task is far from easy.

My experience, though, is that life in the youth department is a tangible micro of the macro. In other words, the problems of church youthwork reflect all the problems of the traditional church, but in a more simplified form. After nine years, I have yet to face a problem in the youth programme which does not have a parallel in the history of the wider church. For a variety of reasons though (to do with size, lack of tradition and the flexibility of the people involved) the problems are more easy to address in the youth ministry context. That is what fuels my sense of urgency in presenting this chapter. For if the Jubilee is a pattern for youth ministry it is most certainly a pattern of ministry for the whole church.

This is important for another reason. Youth ministers have the dubious reputation of being highly critical of the church establishment. If the above argument is accepted, however, whenever this chapter appears to be critical of the traditional church, I am being equally critical of my own work.

Join with me, then, on my journey that has led me over the last eight years to experience one of the key problems of the traditional Western church within the youth ministry setting and see how we have discovered the Jubilee pattern of ministry to have some exciting and possibly far reaching implications for more than just one local church's youth programme.

Foundations

In 1987, I started full time youth ministry at Stopsley Baptist Church and sought to develop a programme based on biblical principles for Christian youth ministry.

It is my conviction that Christian youth ministry is founded on the Bible. It was Mark Ashton who wrote, 'The most serious weakness in the Christian churches, outreach to teenagers today, is not a failure to understand our culture. It is a failure to take the Bible sufficiently seriously.'[2] The Bible's teaching on youthwork is a constant in a sea of change. It is not that I do not read educational policy, or papers on cultural development, but rather I read them in the light of God's revelation through scripture. I believe the Bible to be unchanging, yet dynamic, engaging, yet transcending, any culture.

Obviously, there is no systematic theology of youthwork within the Bible, but there are principles which must be allowed to shape our youthwork practice. Herein lies another chapter, but, stated with extreme brevity, I would see these principles as follows:

⊙ Though God is clearly a God of all ages (Joel 2:28, 29) the Bible does seem to suggest that youth is seen as a group distinct both from adults and children (that is, 1 John 2:12–14).

⊙ The Bible would also seem to suggest that when communicating with this age group there is room for a different approach. (Contrast, for example, the styles in Proverbs 4:1–7 and 22:6 when addressing children and chapter 23 when addressing young people.)

⊙ Far from being 'try to hold on to them' years, adolescence in scripture is both a period of access and achievement in the things of God. (For example, the call narratives of Jeremiah and Samuel plus the examples of David, Joseph, Daniel, Josiah and so on.)

⊙ A theology of youth ministry is anchored in the cross (Galatians 2:20). For church youthwork to be truly Christian it must include regular and systematic calling for young people to recognize the work of Christ on the cross.

⊙ The Bible also goes on to outline clearly methods by which the cross is to be communicated. These include:

  ⊙ one generation communicating with the next (Psalm 78);

  ⊙ parents communicating with their children (Ephesians 6:4);

  ⊙ holistic communication, that is involving the whole person (Deuteronomy 6:5–9);

  ⊙ incarnational communication (1 Thessalonians 2:8; 2 Thessalonians1:5–7); and

  ⊙ cross-cultural communication (Acts 17:16).

It was on this set of priorities, therefore, that we sought to develop our work.

My understanding of Acts 17 led me to believe that the more fundamentally biblical we are, the more radical our expressions of cross-cultural communication can become. It was C. H. Spurgeon who said that the Christian needs a Bible in one hand and a newspaper in the other, and it was in this spirit that we tried to apply our youthwork practice. We undertook regular surveys and on one occasion asked twenty questions of all 3,000 eleven- to sixteen-year-olds in our area.

What we found was that culture's currents were moving very quickly. Not simply at the level of music and fashion, but more importantly at the level of the way people think. A simple example of this would be that, when I started, a fair number of non-Christian teenagers used to enjoy attending our evening service. Within five years, however, despite considerable improvements, Sunday night at church was more than many of our Christian young people could cope with and non-Christians were almost exclusively absent.

Our wider reading of cultural change also served to emphasize a growing isolation and loneliness amongst teenagers, and only served to increase our commitment to incarnational relational youth ministry as being key to our future. So we started to try to engage the young people of our area with our message by seeking to make all our work relationally based, by creating structures that reflected biblical priorities and at the same time drew on all our cultural research to provide large, loud and attractive programmes for teenagers to enjoy. We aimed to be both culturally relevant in the way we ran our programme and culturally engaging in the way we communicated the message of the cross.

Growth

Over the first four or five years we were relatively successful at what we were doing, not only with large numbers in attendance, but more importantly a regular trickle of teenagers coming to faith, and a good proportion of those going on to be committed followers.

Evaluation

Three generations came and went, and patterns of work and relating became established. However, with the fourth generation, I began to feel uncomfortable. Though everything appeared fine from the outside I began to feel that things were not quite right. We commissioned an audit of everything we did, from which several issues became clear.

LACK OF OWNERSHIP

The current youth programme had originated with a previous generation of young people. However hard we tried to get kids to participate, they didn't 'own' it like they used to, it just wasn't theirs. Whatever we tried did not seem to shift the misunderstanding that we were the providers and they were the clients.

A MEANS TO AN END HAD BECOME AN END IN ITSELF

Over the years our desire to be culturally relevant had led to a more and more sophisticated programme, which placed increasing demands on those leading. For youth leaders with full-time jobs, families and other church responsibilities, this meant that quality relational work with teenagers was being squeezed out by time pressures. We only ran a programme to create a context for relationships, but what was designed as a means to an end was fast becoming an end in itself.

COMPLACENCY

We were becoming complacent. We prayed and said we trusted God, but there were times when I wondered if our confidence was based more on our reputation and structures than our experience of a dynamic, living God working amongst us.

NEED FOR CHANGE

There was a felt need for change. We were not seeing people regularly converted as we had done, and we were not seeing large numbers of kids really excited about their faith and obviously growing.

Analysing the problem

Following a period of reflection, I began to realize that what we were experiencing in the youth department was once again a mirror image of what the church has experienced throughout its history, namely institutionalism.

History is full of examples of small groups of believers experiencing spontaneous growth, developing systems to manage that growth, only for the systems to eventually become dominant and stifle the initial vitality and, to my horror, we were no exception. Whether it was the early church until Constantine's conversion, or Luther and the Reformation, Wesley and Methodism, or Booth and the Salvation Army (to name but a few), the experience would appear the same. Indeed, the cynic would say that, judging by more recent church history at least, it takes a denomination about one hundred years to move from being alive and kicking to comatose and twitching!

Rob Warner notes in his book, *Twenty-first Century Church*, how church history is littered with one-generational movements. He quotes the example of Francis of Assissi, whose followers, even before he died, were planning a building in his memory which totally contradicted Assissi's commitment to simplicity! As R. T. Kendall has said, 'History is full of those who have copied the effect, but lost the heart of the cause.'[3]

Not that, by any means, institutionalism is exclusively a church phenomenon. In fact, so established is it throughout human history that the French have a saying for it: 'Plus ça change, plus c'est la même chose.' ('The more it changes, the more it is the same thing!')

Institutionalism is well-recognized, for example, in the world of business. In their book, *In Search of Excellence*, Peters and Waterman talk about staying fresh and vibrant as the key issue for any expanding company. They warn, 'Organization gets paralysed because structures dilute priorities.' They suggest that it is sometimes necessary for a company to 'deacquisition' itself of some of its assets, and get back to the basics of what it does best. The best companies, they argue, branch out and expand, whilst staying close to their core.[4]

Oliver Nyumbu, a management consultant working in Birmingham, has suggested to me that his experience of institutions over the years is that management structures have more to do with managing the anxiety of the 'people at the top' than with getting the job done.

It is perhaps in this management context that Tom Sine's words about the church can be understood: 'We thought we could embrace modernization with all its affluence and benefits without ever being tainted by its values. Belatedly, a few seem to be waking up to the reality that when we welcome modernization into our lives we unwittingly invite secularization into our souls as well.'[5]

Towards a solution

So much for analysis! But what were we to do? I saw that I was party to the church's perennial problem of institutionalism, but what was the way forward? Because of my understanding of Christian youthwork foundations, I went back to the Bible and because of my conviction that the youthworker's task involves crossing cultural barriers, I ended up reading the missionaries' writings on scripture. It was here that I came across the work of Roland Allen.

ROLAND ALLEN

Roland Allen was a missionary in North China about the time of World War 1. His two most prominent works are *The Spontaneous Expansion of the Christian Church* and

Missionary Methods: St Paul's or Ours. Leslie Newbiggin wrote of him, 'Read Roland Allen and your ideas will be questioned by a voice more searching than the word of man.'[6] That was a good enough recommendation for me!

To my amazement, what Allen had experienced at the turn of the century in his missionary work in China was exactly what I was experiencing in youthwork in late twentieth-century England. For example:

Our love of organization leads us to rely upon it. When an organization is set up, growth is logical and mechanical, and it ceases to produce spiritually when it does.

Our organization immobilizes our missionaries. It creates and maintains large stations and great institutions and these absorb a very great proportion of our energy. We cannot move freely.

Continuity is often argued as a plus resulting from organization—in truth, you cannot expect spiritual results from an organization, only from God.

Elaborate organization exercises a strange fascination over the minds of men. It becomes an end in itself. Men incline more and more to rely upon it. They learn to ascribe to it virtues which do not belong to it.

There is a horrible tendency for an organization to grow in importance until it overshadows the end of its existence and begins to exist for itself.[7]

Roland Allen pointed me to an alternative model of church organization, through his study of Acts in *The Spontaneous Expansion of the Christian Church.* He argued that if the church in China (which the missionaries were seeking to plant) was to be truly indigenous, it must spring up in indigenous soil from the very first seed planted. He argued that it was biblically compromising to have indigenous churches ruled by foreign missionaries and that it only led to sterility and resentment. 'Our method has a strong restraining influence. We pray for God to fill our converts with zeal and then shrink back from the steps which would encourage this. We fear human self assertion too much.'[8]

Allen argued from Acts that the early church's story was prescriptive, not descriptive, on the basis that there has never been a time since when the church has grown as strongly or as quickly. Using passages such as Acts 8:4, 16:3 and 1 Thessalonians 1:8, Allen argued that you cannot have spontaneous expansion and total control. Spontaneous expression is the only way to spontaneous expansion and that seemingly unorganized activity will always be efficient if it is ordained by God.

To illustrate this point he used the example of Madagascar. Between 1870 and 1895 all the missionaries were expelled. Given that they were leading the church, one would naturally assume that church numbers would dwindle as a result. In fact what happened was entirely the opposite; the church grew by ten times its original number! In 1875 when the missionaries returned, however, they immediately set about constructing churches, hospitals and schools that would service the growth. The growth stopped. Institutionalism had set in once again.

Michael Harper, in his book *Let My People Grow*, goes on to quote the example of China. In 1949, when the missionaries were expelled, China had approximately one million Christians. In their absence and despite persecution, the church grew at an incredible rate. By 1987 conservative estimates put the figure in excess of 50 million.

I had always been taught that persecution led to greater commitment and that is why persecuted churches flourished, but now I began to see something else. Though greater commitment undeniably played an important part, another factor was at work. Persecution by nature forced the cessation of organized religious activity. I saw that vibrant faith freed from the shackles of religious institutionalism acted as a powerful recipe for growth.

Such a spontaneous model was contrary to much of what I had previously thought, and flew in the face of Western institutionalism, but the more I read the book of Acts the more I became convinced that the more thoroughly biblical we are, the more radical and trusting our models of ecclesiology become.

So far, so good. I was inspired and invigorated by Allen's work, but my problem was how to get from here to there!

How could we take a highly developed youth programme, which had fallen into the client/provider mentality of institutionalism, into a spontaneous flexible model which the young people once again owned and directed?

It was during my reading of Mark Senter's book, *The Coming Revolution in Youth Ministry*, that I had what some would call my 'Aha moment'.[9] It was just one throw-away line regarding a youthworker suggesting a year of Jubilee for his organization that suddenly hit me. Perhaps there was in scripture an answer to the perennial problem of institutionalism... the year of Jubilee.

The year of Jubilee

Leviticus 25 outlines the key points of the year of Jubilee as follows:

⊙ It was to happen every fifty years in the life of the nation of Israel.

⊙ Everyone was to return to their own property (verse 13).

⊙ Everyone was to return acquired properties to their original owners (verse 31).

⊙ The Israelites were not to sow any crops for the year and live by faith (verse 11 and verse 21).

⊙ People were to release their slaves (verse 54).

⊙ It was to act as a regular economic leveller in the life of the nation of Israel (verse 16).

The question is, why did God call the Israelites to take such a radical step? The key is in Leviticus 25:55. 'For the Israelites belong to me as servants. They are my servants who I have brought out of Egypt. I am the Lord your God.' In other words, the Jubilee did away with much of the trappings of sophisticated national status and the infrastructure of the emerging nation, and took Israel back to the simple trust of a nomadic wandering people. God did not want Israel to lose that sense of dependency and be like the other nations. Fundamentally, the question the Jubilee addressed was: Where is your trust and security—in God, or in your nation's structures?

Hermeneutically speaking, Leviticus 25 can be understood in two ways for us today as we battle with institutionalized Christianity:

PRINCIPLE TRANSFER

In the same way that Israel was asked to give up its structures to help it get back to what it was intended to be, so the church must view its structures as slaves not masters, dispensable immediately they cease to serve the cause of the gospel.

IMAGE

Sharon Runge, in her book *Jesus, Liberation and Biblical Jubilee*, says this of image: 'Images, though rooted in particular contexts and though tentative and elastic, have the power nevertheless to change one's world... form reality and bridge traditionally separate areas of life.'

It was precisely this Jubilee image that Isaiah picked up to describe the work of the coming Messiah and it was those words steeped in Jubilee imagery which Jesus adopted as his own in Luke 4:18,19. 'The spirit of the Lord is on me, because he has anointed me to preach good news to the poor. He has sent me to proclaim freedom for the prisoners and recovery of the sight for the blind, to release the oppressed, to proclaim the year of the Lord's favour.'

It is this image of liberation which Jubilee captures and in doing so breathes both challenge and hope into traditional church structures.

Thrilled with the possibility that there was a radical biblical model to move from a Western institutionalized approach in youth ministry to a more spontaneous Acts-like model through the inauguration of a Jubilee year, we decided to experiment. Not that the decision was undertaken lightly. As the reader might imagine, with so many people having worked for so long on the youth programme, we all needed convincing that we were not just throwing all that effort away. It took three months. Three months of questioning and evaluation. Three months of people feeling confused and insecure. Some understandably reacted angrily against it, feeling that it was naive and irresponsible, a vote of 'No confidence' in the youth leaders who had worked so hard in previous years. The same ground was travelled over time after time. 'It is not that structures are wrong, but programme must always flow from relationships, never replace them,' I heard myself saying, time after time. To be honest, there were times when I felt dreadfully inadequate because I couldn't 'get' people to understand. There were times when I felt exasperated by the speed of the decision-making process; times of feeling incredibly excited as some began to grasp what we were talking about. Overwhelmingly, though, I felt helpless. This was such a big decision, I could not ask people just to go along with it. Each individual had to know that this was of God. Suffice to say that after long deliberation there was unanimous agreement that we should try this way forward. On 1 June 1994 we therefore suspended our formal youth programme.

In practice this meant closing our organized meetings and instead encouraging informal and flexible friendship networks between youthworkers and small groups of young people. We wanted to wrest the initiative away from structures and programmes, and back into incarnational relationships.

THE PROBLEMS OF A JUBILEE STYLE MINISTRY

Almost immediately problems began to emerge. Perhaps they can be summarized as follows:

The Jubilee image refuses to be packaged

You cannot tie down an image. Everybody wanted clear answers to clear questions, that is: How long will it last? What are you going to do in the meantime? How are you going to organize your youth leaders? and so on, and so on. Whereas before we had always had an answer, or at least found an answer, it was incredibly difficult to say 'I don't know', without sounding hugely irresponsible. The truth was it would be very easy just to organize another programme, but we were determined not to respond to pressure and allow God to lead us.

The pressure of expectancy

Overnight all the gloss and the glitz of an apparently successful youth programme disappeared. There was a very strong underlying expectation that the Jubilee needed to produce some tangible fruit and produce quickly if people were to be convinced, but the Jubilee was all about building long-term foundations, not producing instant success.

The pressure of communication

Overnight a highly visible youth programme went underground. Small groups of teenagers meeting at youth leaders' houses or going shopping together and so on were not visible in the way the Express Bar or the holiday clubs had been. Almost immediately there were some good things going on, but most people did not see them any more.

The pressure of misunderstanding

What quickly became obvious through peoples' questions was that the wider church, and especially the parents, had confused a means to an end with an end in itself. 'When are we going to start doing youthwork again?' reflected a major breakdown in understanding. If one defines Christian youthwork as adults entering into the world of a teenager and making Jesus known, then the Jubilee saw us arguably doing more youthwork than we had ever done before. The majority, however, did not see it like that!

The pressure of unlearning

The trouble is that the Jubilee challenges old ways of doing things. As youth leaders we are finding that we are having to change some of our previous working practices and, in particular, our desire to organize and arrange things for young people. Perhaps one of the most difficult things that we have had to unlearn is that being vulnerable and not knowing what we are going to do next is not necessarily a bad thing!

The pressure of a continuing church programme

The church leadership, whilst supporting the youth department's Jubilee, did not feel it was appropriate for the wider church. This obviously caused problems as we were still required to 'do something' with young people on a Sunday morning, for example, and youth leaders were still required to be part of house groups and so on. What we soon found was that we needed to meet more regularly as a team for prayer and teaching, but such were the demands placed on a youth leader's personal resources that the burden of time became impossible. In the end, the youth leadership team began to meet as a house group.

The pressure of not enough youth leaders

Almost half of our forty youth leaders, though agreeing with Jubilee in theory, decided that it was a good time for them personally to leave the team. I think they felt exposed without a programme to work within (despite all the training we provided) and several confided in me that they realized that (despite what they had previously said) their own personal relationship with God was simply not strong enough. We quickly became short-staffed.

The pressure of declining numbers

Without a glitzy programme to attract any more, the initial result of the Jubilee is a decline in attendance of those young people who are not Christians or enquiring about faith.

As we have begun to communicate Jubilee with others, four other problems have emerged.

A rallying point for the disenchanted

I am very wary of those who are critical of the Western church without being constructive in that criticism. I am anxious that the Jubilee message is not hijacked by those who are more frustrated than positive. Inevitably, the Jubilee is critical of many of our religious institutions, but I would remind the reader of my earlier comments. If this chapter ever points a finger at the wider church, there are four more pointed back at me. The focus of my writing is not to be harsh on the Western church, rather it is simply to remind us all that the church of Jesus Christ is a means to an end, not an end in itself. The church exists to see God's kingdom come. The purpose of the Jubilee is to see people in their thousands experiencing the life-transforming message of the gospel, not to slate the church. As Chuck Kraft has said: 'The traditional Western church are truly God's people, but as for me, my heart is for the 90 per cent of people who will not traditionalize in order to become Christian.'[10]

It can be a glorious cop-out

At first glance, Jubilee can sound more like anarchy and be seen as very naive and idealistic as a result. That is not what I believe it is about. Revolution is always so much more attractive than reformation to those who are frustrated. However, I identify very much with what David Sheppard wrote in *Built as a City*:

The Institutional church need constantly to be reformed, so that they actually serve people, rather than simply maintain their life. Such reform needs the vision of those who have perhaps seen the system's failures most clearly because they have stepped outside it. Some will find they can serve within such institutions; others can bring pressure to bear on them. What they cannot afford to do, if they really want the well being of the big city, is to write off the institutions, or to believe that a revolution which destroys the whole system will by magic produce a better life. Revolution is only another sort of withdrawal, because it refuses to attempt the hard grind of working out, persuading and sustaining the real policies which help real people.[11]

I am not suggesting for one moment that the Jubilee is this kind of withdrawal or a panacea for all ills, nor that it is the only answer for institutionalism.

It is critical to understand, however, that, far from being irresponsible, the Jubilee actually takes, not abdicates, responsibility. I would argue that the charge of irresponsibility must surely be faced by those who plod on amending proven failed systems of church structures when more radical changes are required. When less than 10 per cent of the population regularly attend church and we simply tinker with the times of our services, that really is irresponsibility! It is simply rearranging the deckchairs on the Titanic. Just how bad do things have to get? 'The history of the church is the history of the subversion of Christianity from within, compromised by culture and conventional human religion. What we need is not modest adaption, but a radical overhaul of traditional doctrine of the church. In Christ is found the abolition of human religion.'[12]

Too simple and idealistic

In the face of the complexities of institutionalism, I recognize that the Jubilee concept can at first appear to be incredibly simple. In response, I would say two things:

First, though a concept in itself may be simple to grasp, that does not necessarily mean that its implementation will be easy. There is little evidence that Israel ever fully carried out the detail of Leviticus 25, presumably for precisely this reason—it was hugely costly and difficult to do. As G. K. Chesterton has put it, 'The Christian ideal has not been tried and found wanting, it has been found difficult and left untried.' One can only hope that God's people have learnt the lessons of history as to the cost of ignoring his instructions!

Second, this chapter is not prescribing a methodology. We may have suspended our programme, but for others the Jubilee may equally involve the complicated discerning process of establishing what of our church life and structure is vibrant and focused for today, and what is unnecessary baggage from yesterday. In short, the difference between tradition (the living faith of the dead) and traditionalism (the dead faith of the living). Another church I heard of only recently has inaugurated some Jubilee Sundays and weeks into its calendar, where services are cancelled and replaced by fellowship meals and so on, as its response to the challenge of Jubilee.

The critical question is, of course, where do we place our trust? If we are prepared to face that one honestly and not sidestep the issues that Leviticus 25 raises, whatever the process we thereafter adopt, it is sure to be beneficial.

The Jubilee was always bad news for the rich

Leviticus 25 was great news for slaves and the dispossessed, but it was always bad news for the powerful and rich, those who had prospered under the institutional system. Throughout history those who have proposed radical change to the church (even when it has been desperately needed) have always faced their greatest opposition from those within the church who have inherited power from within its structures. Even in seemingly unimportant changes, great criticism has been reserved for those who implement them. For example, Wesley was banned from many Anglican pulpits simply for preaching in the open air. Sadly, history repeats itself and anybody seriously advocating a Jubilee to the institutional church will meet similar opposition. However, as Roland Allen wrote: 'There is an urgency for each generation to submit afresh the traditions of men to the Word and Spirit of God. One day, someone will see that action is demanded and perhaps screw up their courage and take it.'[13]

THE ADVANTAGES OF THE JUBILEE

A biblical model
Exegetes of Leviticus 25 have tended to focus on the issue of social justice. Important though it is, I would suggest its success flows from the nation being asked first to put its trust and security in God alone—only then, when trust is in God and not in material things, will real, genuine, sacrificial giving occur. I firmly believe that Leviticus 25 is a biblical challenge to Western Christianity's institutional church.

Structures that embody God's sovereignty
The Jubilee pattern of ministry ensures that we hold on to our structures less seriously and keep them as a means to an end rather than allowing them to become an end in themselves. It was Tennyson who said:

> Our little systems have their day.
> They have their day and cease to be.
> They are but broken lights of Thee
> And Thou Oh Lord art more than they.

Leviticus 25, taken seriously, would leave the church of Jesus Christ with all the flexibility of a movement, not the sterility of an institution.

It provides flexibility
Everything we hear about the new paradigm in culture says that we must be more imaginative in responding to tomorrow's challenges and that before we can meaningfully think about cultural engagement we must first address our own cultural entrapment. 'The church is so encumbered with its own institutionalization that it can't reach the community it is called to serve.'[14]

For example, take the institutional churches' response to industrialization in nineteenth-century Britain. Dunkerfield in Lancashire grew to 10,000 inhabitants before it had its first Anglican church and by then the town had no less than seventeen non-conformist churches![15] Jubilee addresses this need for flexibility and loosens the ropes that hold back the church.

Movement
The Jubilee addresses one of the key problems of cultural engagement, namely that it is a constantly moving target. What is relevant one minute is apparently irrelevant the next. We live in a world which is constantly reinventing itself. 'Technology creates a culture and constantly reformulates it for its own market ends. Youth culture will never stabilize as the ad man will always have another product to sell.'[16]

Just when we begin to catch up with the post war world, bringing the sound of popular music into the mainstream of our worship, we realize that our culture has entered a new era of video and multi media entertainment, communication and information exchange.[17]

In a world like this, change has to be a permanent feature of church life and Jubilee helps encourage this mentality.

It encourages new leadership
It was Mark Senter who, in writing about the coming revolution in youth ministry, said, 'The key to this revolution is not the ability of the current generation to adapt, but its capacity to relinquish leadership to a new paradigm of leaders.'[18]

What we have found in our practice of the Jubilee is that it acts as a rallying call for ownership and participation in the activities of the youth programme. We are discovering new parameters of working that go beyond adults answering questions for young people or simply trying to entertain. We are beginning to experience the first signs of a 'we are in this together' mentality, the first fruits of a new generation of young people emerging into leadership.

An idea whose time has come

The Jubilee concept seems to tie together many emerging strands of different Christian groups. Whether it is academics like Graham Cray calling for dramatic changes in our ecclesiology in response to post-modernism; whether it is the pragmatic evangelists like the Willow Creek Church or Alpha groups modelling significant changes in the way we do things; whether it is the charismatics suspending their existing programmes in response to what has been labelled the 'Toronto blessing,' or an increasing number of experiments with youth congregations or churches, there does seem to be an emerging picture of loosening the traditional approaches to church.

It brings liberation and hope

We often talk of the importance of hope in Christian experience today. In the same way as the first Jubilee was designed to bring liberation and hope to the slaves of Israel, so today the Jubilee principles and imagery are a symbol of hope, not only to the thousands of Christians who feel their church experience is an irrelevant time warp, but also to the 90 per cent of people in the Western world who will not traditionalize in order to become Christian.

Conclusion

I look forward to the day when we will see tens of thousands of people from outside the church tradition coming to faith in Christ, but before this happens there has to be a far greater mission-focused flexibility to our ecclesiological structures. In that sense, the Jubilee message is a forerunner to us truly experiencing 'The year of the Lord's favour'.

> *A time of Jubilee is coming... where old and young will turn to Jesus.*
>
> *Swing wide you heavenly gates, prepare the way of the risen Lord.*[19]

It is with that unashamed hope of revival that I write this chapter, crying to church leaders today the words of the prophet of old... 'Let my people go'.

NOTES

1. Michael Eastman, *Inside Out: A Handbook for Youth Leaders*, Falcon, p. 127.

2. Mark Ashton, *Christian Youthwork*, Kingsway.

3. R. T. Kendall, Sermon at Stopsley Baptist Church, Autumn 1993 .

4. Peters and Waterman, *In Search of Excellence*, p. 305.

5. Tom Sine, *Wild Hope*, Monarch, p. 207.

6. Lesslie Newbegin in foreword to *Missionary Methods: St Paul's or Ours?* by Roland Allen, Eerdmans.

7. Roland Allen, *The Spontaneous Expansion Of the Christian Church*, pp. 131–133.

8. Allen, *The Spontaneous Expansion*.

9. Mark Senter, *The Coming Revolution In Youth Ministry*, p. 162.

10. Chuck Kraft.

11. David Sheppard, *Built As A City*.

12. Rob Warner, *Twenty First Century Church*, Hodder & Stoughton, p. 139.

13. Allen, *Missionary Methods*, p. 1.

14. Rob Frost.

15. Warner, *Twenty First Century Church*.

16. Schultz, Q., Anker, R., Bratt, J., Romanowski, W., Worst, J. and Zuidervaart, L., *Dancing in the Dark: Youth, Popular Culture and the Electronic Media*, Eerdmans, 1991.

17. Schultz, *Dancing in the Dark*.

18. Mark Senter, 'Historic Perspective of Children/Youth Ministers and World Evangelization', 1992 ELMA Mission Executive Retreat, Glen Eyrie, Colorado Springs.

19. Martin Smith, *Do You Feel the Mountains Tremble?*, Cutting Edge 3.